MUSICAL THEATRE

GERRY TEBBUTT

EDITED BY

JOHN NICHOLAS AND KEN PICKERING

DRAMATIC LINES, TWICKENHAM, ENGLAND
Musical Theatre
text copyright © Gerry Tebbutt 2003

Dramatic Lines
PO Box 201
Twickenham
TW2 5RQ
England

A CIP record for this book is
available from the British Library

ISBN 1 904557 12 0

Musical Theatre
first published in 2003
by
Dramatic Lines
Twickenham England

Printed by The Dramatic Lines Press
Twickenham England

FOREWORD

This **MUSICAL THEATRE Handbook** is one of a series primarily designed to support students and teachers preparing for examinations from the Drama and Speech syllabus of Trinity College, *London*.

However, the Dramatic Lines Handbooks have much wider applications. Not only do they provide accessible and practical advice to students working towards ANY examination in Drama, Speech, Communication or Performing Arts, they also give invaluable help to those who wish to use their skills in a professional capacity as performers, teachers or communicators.

The Handbooks are quite literally something to keep to hand whenever you are working towards an important examination, performance, audition or presentation and you will find that they become your constant companions for a life in the Performance and Communications Arts.

Ken Pickering

Ken Pickering

Chief Examiner for Drama and Speech at
Trinity College, *London* and Professor of Arts Education
at the Institute for Arts in Therapy and Education

For Richard Fraser and Jill Francis

"We said we wouldn't look back."

Salad Days (Julian Slade, 1954)

INTRODUCTION

For many of us, seeing a musical production in a theatre transports us to a make-believe world. We thrill to the magic . . . . from that spine-tingling moment when the orchestra has finished tuning up, the house lights are lowered and the overture begins.

Then the curtain rises and for two hours or more we follow a story that is told by acting, singing and dance.

The show might have a strong, emotional story supported by a wonderful score and good lyrics that stay inside your head long after the curtain has come down. Perhaps the story has additional visual elements of excitement – a crashing chandelier, a helicopter or a flying car! Maybe the production includes wonderful ensemble work and exciting choreography or even a star performer.

There are those who have a passion for theatre and seek more than passive audience involvement. These are the people who want to live their lives in the world of musical theatre . . . . .

CONTENTS

INTRODUCTION

1   YOU WANT TO BE IN MUSICALS   1

   A changing theatre industry   2

   Television talent shows   3

   Working in the entertainment industry   4

   The triple threat performer   5

   Grades and examinations   6

   Becoming a performer – what is involved?   8

2   CHOOSING A DRAMA SCHOOL COURSE   15

   How do I find a course to suit me?   18

   Is the course recognised?

   What next? – I've looked at the prospectuses   19

   Open days   22

   Short courses   23

   Private visits

3   STARTING TO PREPARE FOR YOUR AUDITION   25

4   CHOOSING SUITABLE SONGS   27

   Researching a song   28

   Finding your own style   29

   Speeches leading into songs

   The suitability of material   30

   Presentation of a song   32

   The choice of songs available   33

   Discarded material   34

5	TYPES AND STYLES OF SONG	36
	❖ BALLAD	
	❖ UP-TEMPO	38
	❖ PATTER	39
	❖ TORCH AND ANTHEMIC	40
	❖ COMEDY	41
	❖ POINT NUMBER	43
	❖ ROCK	45
	❖ POP	46
	❖ OPERETTA	47
	❖ CLASSICAL	49
	❖ BELT	50
	❖ CHARACTER	53
	❖ PASTICHE	55
	❖ PARLOUR	57
	❖ BLUES	58
	❖ SONG AND DANCE	60
	❖ MUSIC-HALL	61

6	ORIGINS OF SONGS AND STAGE MUSICALS	62
	Classical material	63
	The works of Shakespeare	64
	Screen musicals	65

7	PREPARING YOUR AUDITION MATERIAL	67
	The next steps	
	The elements of your voice	69
	Breathing and phrasing	

	Gestures	70
	Accents	71
	Songs taken out of context	
	Compilation books	72
	Props	73
	Sheet music	74
	Do I need an accompanist?	76
	The Musical Director	77
8	PREPARING YOUR AUDITION SPEECH	78
	At your audition	80
9	PREPARING FOR YOUR DANCE AUDITION	83
	Memory training	84
	The dance tutor	85
10	THE DAY OF YOUR AUDITION	86
	Dress do's and don'ts	
	Feeling unwell	88
11	YOUR INTERVIEW	89
	What is the panel is looking for?	94
	Who's on the panel?	97
	Suppose I'm not offered a place?	98
	Feedback	99
	Interview pitfalls	100
12	A POTTED HISTORY OF THE MUSICAL	103

Styles of musical   104

13   YOU HAVE ARRIVED AT DRAMA SCHOOL   115
      What now?
      Investing in your course
      Punctuality and discipline   117
      Classes   118

14   NOW YOU HAVE GRADUATED   122
      Losing focus and determination   123
      Performers that get the jobs   124
      You audition but don't get the job   125

15   THE WORLD OF MUSICALS   126
      WHERE TO GO FOR MORE HELP   127
      BIBLIOGRAPHY   129

1 YOU WANT TO BE IN MUSICALS

So, you want to be in musicals.

Q Why?

I suppose many of us, at one time or another, have felt the urge to be in a musical. Maybe we've dreamed of what it must be like to float down a stairway and into a room – to meet our partner and take off in song and dance, after watching an old Fred Astaire and Ginger Rogers movie on a Sunday afternoon.

Your daydream might have been triggered by watching Gene Kelly dance with Judy Garland or John Travolta and Olivia Newton-John gyrating in *Grease* – or possibly Patrick Swayze provided the inspiration in *Dirty Dancing*.

Alternatively you might have elected to dream of playing Velma, Roxy or Billy Flynn in *Chicago* or perhaps you have seen an inspirational production of *Fame* or *West Side Story* and now feel an urgent need to be onstage as a member of a musical theatre company.

Maybe you thought how wonderful it must feel to be part of the magic lands inhabited by characters like Cinderella, Snow White or Aladdin as a small child seeing your first Christmas show, Disney film or pantomime.

Whatever the motivation, you have decided that you want to be part of the magical make-believe world of musical theatre . . . . . but it is much more difficult to achieve your dream than you imagine.

A changing theatre industry

The theatre industry has changed rapidly over the last few years; and the breakdown and disintegration of regional theatres throughout the world means far fewer jobs for those entering the profession.

The accessibility and popularity of holidays abroad has had far reaching consequences in England. Once upon a time there were theatres in all of the seaside resorts that presented full-scale summer shows or summer stock but these have now almost disappeared.

Q What is left?

Now, only a few regional theatres remain which occasionally do a musical production. In addition there are some 'number one' – and, very often, 'number two' tours, one-night stands and shows on cruise liners or in holiday camps.

Of course the major influences for musical theatre can still be seen in the West End of London and on New York's Broadway and these productions often get picked up and produced in theatres in the major cities throughout the world.

Television talent shows

Even television variety shows have become a thing of the past. As a performer trying to get a break you will probably find yourself in competition with participants from television talent shows like the recent UK *Popstars* and *Fame Academy* – and all the similar shows that are likely to follow in the future.

"Hearsay", the first manufactured singing group to emerge from a UK television 'talent' show, crashed and failed miserably after eighteen months. The group had fame and celebrity for a short spell but unfortunately not a lasting career in the entertainment industry.

Television talent shows of this type are not so much

to do with talent as immediate image and instant celebrity. If that is what you want then perhaps talent shows of this type are the right playing field for you and there would be little point in continuing reading this book!

However, if you want an interest or a career that is going to last a lifetime . . . . . then read on and discover a number of things about yourself and lots of things about the performing arts industry that should help you achieve your goal.

The ideas that I've set out should not only help you in gaining your place at drama school but also serve as an audition guide when you are out there in the profession or working towards your diploma.

Working in the entertainment industry

The good news is that the theatre does re-invent itself. We should all look forward to the time when theatre flourishes again; not only in major cities but also in the smaller towns around the world that once boasted, and were proud of, their very own theatre.

If you find this depressing then read no further! If you want to stick with it and you are completely motivated and captivated by the entertainment industry and all that it has to offer, then, let us look at your situation objectively and find out what your chances are of succeeding.

If you had wanted to be a carpenter you would have needed to understand how to use certain tools, know about the different types of wood, and be proficient in mathematics and joinery.

However, you have decided to become a performer.

Q How much do you know and understand about the industry that you want to enter?

Q How much do you know about the way your voice works and how to protect it?

Q How much do you know about breathing and your spoken and singing voice?

Q How much do you know about your physical capabilities and stamina?

The triple threat performer

In the early days of musical theatre a large company

was made up of singers who 'just sang' and dancers who 'just danced'; but nowadays, many musical productions require a type of performer known as the 'triple threat performer'.

A triple threat performer is someone who can act and sing and dance - sometimes all at once! It is vital, for yourself and also for the industry that you are able to embrace all three disciplines, in order to survive.

Presenting yourself as a triple threat provides you with more options and increases your chances of success because it affords the opportunity of getting work as an actor, singer or dancer or indeed any combination of the three!

Grades and examinations

If you are going to get the maximum enjoyment and success from your involvement in musical theatre, it is vital that you constantly develop your knowledge, skill and understanding.

An ideal way to do this is to prepare for one of the Grade or Certificate examinations in Musical Theatre offered by Trinity College, *London.*

These examinations are open to everyone and may be taken by individuals, pairs or groups at local centres throughout the English-speaking world. The examinations provide a very helpful guide to your progress and an opportunity to have your work assessed by an independent expert.

If you are seriously considering a professional career in musical theatre and have reached Grade 8, you will have achieved a standard appropriate for an audition for entry to a drama school full-time course.

Even if this is not your intention, you could still continue with your part-time study and work towards one of the Trinity diplomas in Musical Theatre.

The **Associate Diploma** is of a standard equivalent to one year of full-time training and the **Licentiate** represents the standard achieved after three years. A growing number of drama schools are now using these diplomas as additional qualifications for their students.

NOTE: Most of the advice given in this book is phrased as if you are working towards a drama school audition. However, all the advice is just as applicable when applied to any diploma or grade examination – so you mustn't stop reading because you think you are unlikely to take up full-time training!

Becoming a performer – what is involved?

You have the necessary desire and passion to be a performer. It is time to sit down, think seriously about the long journey you are about to embark on, and ask yourself a few questions.

Q Do you need to perform professionally?

Q Would working with amateur companies be enough to satisfy your need?

Let us look at a few points and face facts:

- Many students who graduate from drama school find it difficult to get work. Therefore, in order to keep practising their skills they sometimes become involved in a "profit share" production.

There is nothing wrong with profit share productions except that the people involved probably won't make very much money. Also, unless they are lucky enough to find themselves in a terrific production that grabs the attention of casting directors, agents and potential employers, it isn't really going to enhance their career.

However, involvement in a profit share production will help performers to use their craft and allow them to put their skills into practice.

- Some students find themselves in work situations described as "semi-professional jobs".

There really is no such word as semi-professional – if you are professional you are paid, if you are not professional, therefore amateur, you are not!

- Even though you might have finished your training it is important to keep the training going by continuing dance, drama and singing classes after you have graduated.

- It is also important to go to the theatre as often as you can in order to keep up with current trends.

You must see the work of new writers and new composers and lyricists, directors, choreographers and musical directors and ACTORS, of course.

An actor NEVER stops learning the trade and should be receptive to new ideas, new skills and new methods of acting.

Q If you want to work professionally do you think you have what it takes to become an all round singer, dancer and actor in order to compete?

Neither singing encores in a karaoke bar to rapturous applause nor getting rave reviews in the local papers for your one appearance in an amateur musical production necessarily means that you will have the talent for a career in musical theatre.

Just as dancing in a nightclub doesn't automatically mean that you have what it takes physically to become a good dancer in the entertainment industry.

Let's face it, these singing and dancing skills need a vital additional element – ACTING TALENT!

Q Do you have the tenacity, endurance and determination to put yourself through three years, or the equivalent, of vigorous training at Drama School?

Q Can you face the possibility of having your security blanket (your talent and in some cases personality) stripped away and reshaped and remodelled?

A lot of students arrive at drama schools with bad habits known as "baggage". You have to accept that your tutors will be unloading the "baggage" and replacing it with tried and tested formulas on how to act, sing and dance properly!

Q Do you have the discipline to completely immerse yourself in your training?

The discipline I am talking about is your own personal discipline – self discipline. i.e. making sure that you are wide awake and ready for work at 9.00 a.m. (the time most drama schools commence lessons); and that your brain is ready and eager to accept, digest and receive continual information until the end of the day.

Q Are you aware of the competition that you are going to face?

This starts the day you audition for drama school. You might have been the leading light of your local amateur company or dance school; or your friends and family might have told you that you possess a wealth of talent and that you have what it takes to be a star.

On the day of your audition, I suggest you look around and see who really possesses the talent – it might not be you!

Q   Are you absolutely sure that musical theatre is the right pathway to take?

You may feel passionate about performing in musicals, but perhaps your voice is never going to be good enough or your dance strong enough to turn you into a triple threat performer!

This is not to say that you can't be trained to a certain level in these disciplines but you have to realise that, at a later date, you will need to have the skills to compete with those who do.

If you have a facility in one of the three disciplines and it is your strong point I would suggest that you follow a course that is going to make that particular discipline sensational.

You may be have the potential to be a good actor and you could waste three years of training on a musical theatre course if you simply don't have the aptitude for singing or dance.

Therefore, if your strength lies in acting, it might be a better idea to choose a course that will enhance your acting ability. You will probably get dance/movement and singing classes on an acting course but to a lesser extent than you would on a musical theatre course.

If you have a skill as a dancer perhaps it would be wiser to follow a dance course in order to make that particular skill as profiled as you can.

In addition to the tuition that specialises in drama and dance there are also many courses available that concentrate on the singing voice.

If you specialise in only one discipline this doesn't necessarily mean that you WON'T work.

However, this does mean that you might only be cast in productions that require a particular skill and you will not be able to take advantage of the great variety of opportunities afforded to a triple threat.

Ask yourself these two very important questions:

Q Do I want to perform?

Q Do I need to perform?

If you only *want* to perform then you are perhaps not as passionate as you first thought. If you *need* to perform it means that you are hungry enough to consider training as a possibility and that you would move hell and high water in order to be able to do so.

Q Are you prepared to face rejection?

This is arguably the most important question.

However, if you feel that you can't face rejection, don't worry. Drama school training will teach you how; and once you arrive in the profession you will get used to negative responses very quickly.

If you've answered all these questions, still feel very positive, and haven't changed your mind about your future career, then read on ....

2   CHOOSING A DRAMA SCHOOL COURSE

The next step of your journey will require time, study and, eventually, money. You've definitely decided on a drama training. Therefore, your first task is to start searching around for a course that is going to answer all your needs.

Be selective.

Q   Is it an acting course, a singing or dancing course or a musical theatre course that you need?

Selecting the right training is the most important decision you will make before embarking upon your career in the performing arts.

There are an enormous number of training establishments around the world – some good, some bad and some indifferent. Then there are additional factors that you might wish to take into consideration when choosing a drama school – for example, a number of institutions are very large and others may be a great distance away from where you live.

Perhaps you feel a university drama degree course would be right for you – although these tend to concentrate more on academic work than practical application.

You need to consider what is right for you.

⇨ Most courses follow the academic year and begin in September. Ideally, you should start your search at least a year before, in order to give yourself time to gather all the necessary information.

There are different types of courses available:

> full-time courses

> part-time courses

> postgraduate courses

The majority of full-time courses are three years in length. In addition, there are a number of one year postgraduate courses for those who have had previous training and want to use the course as a 'top up' or feel the need for a more practical course after university. There are also part-time courses available that enable students to have a more flexible pattern of training over a period of several years.

There are many different patterns of training and study emerging now because of the economic pressures of being a student.

You need to find out what your local dance or drama teachers are offering and you should also look at the publicity from drama schools to see what courses are available. In addition to this you must scour the pages of *The Stage* newspaper for training information.

Many drama schools run degree courses as well as diploma courses. You might ask yourself if a degree offers more chances of employment. The answer is NO - it doesn't.

However, in terms of a wider understanding of the industry that you want to be part of, it is a good thing to have a degree and it will come in useful when you face those lean times in your career.

The skills that you acquire from a drama school training can be transferred to other areas of the acting profession. Such as: becoming an agent, providing training courses for the business sector, entering the teaching profession, public speaking or developing your entrepreneurial skills for setting up and running your own company.

Even if you don't manage to get work in the industry, a drama school training will help you in most other areas of your working life.

How do I find a course to suit me?

 Start by obtaining prospectuses.

 You could also try these useful UK web sites:

> ➢ NCDT (National Council for Drama Training)
> www.ncdt.co.uk

> ➢ CDS (Conference of Drama Schools)
> www.drama.ac.uk

> ➢ CDET (Council for Dance Education)
> www.cdet.org.uk

These organisations can also inform you about courses for which you may be able to obtain a grant, to help towards the cost of your training.

Is the course recognised?

Not only is the Internet a useful tool to search for schools and colleges where you can train but it also offers you the opportunity find out whether a course you are interested in is overseen by an exterior body that ensures the school or college is supplying and carrying out what it says in the prospectus.

It would be advisable for you to choose a course that

has a nationally recognised profile where the training, not only adheres to what is written in the prospectus and in the mission statements, but also has teaching methods and an ideology that are supported by practitioners within the industry.

 Trinity College, *London*, is the awarding body for the qualifications gained by students on a number of leading Dance, Drama and Musical Theatre courses.

What next? – I've looked at the prospectuses

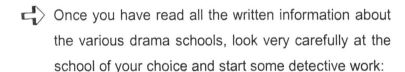 Once you have read all the written information about the various drama schools, look very carefully at the school of your choice and start some detective work:

- Does the school that you are interested in have any kudos within the industry?

- What is the ethos and mission statement of the school?

- What does the school claim to be able to do for you?

- Does the school offer film, television and radio training?

- Will you have the opportunity of meeting or working with potential employers?

- Find out who is on the faculty and look at their professional and teaching profile.

- Find out who trained at the school of your choice and look at their professional career and successes.

- Find out whether the elements offered on the course are going to enhance your performance qualities and give you the right training in the areas that you need.

- Does the school have a policy of master classes that would provide you with the opportunity and experience of working with leading directors, choreographers or actors?

- Will the school ultimately showcase your talent to agents and casting directors and launch you into the profession?

- Does the school provide a careers officer to help you to understand and guide you through the network of agents and casting directors?

- Will the school's careers officer help you prepare your professional c.v. and photographs, and introduce you to the world of the theatre?

- Does the course concentrate on one particular discipline and give little emphasis to the others?

If you want to become a triple threat the emphasis should be equal on the three disciplines – acting, singing and dancing. See if you can get hold of a timetable and see what classes are offered.

If you have the resources, try to see at least one of the drama school productions.

This will give you an idea of the standard that might be expected of you. Also, you will be able to see the standard of students who are well into their training.

A good school doesn't want your money – it wants your talent!

I have known of schools that have offered places over the telephone without seeing the applicant – I wonder what schools like that are interested in?

Open days

Many drama schools run open days – so ring up and find out when they are and, if possible, try to attend. This will help you get a flavour of the establishment; you might see some class work or rehearsals taking place and might find an opportunity to talk to some of the students about their courses.

You should:

> ➢ Ask questions about the training.

> ➢ Ask questions about the school.

> ➢ Ask questions about the staff.

Q Is the school empowering the students with confidence?

Q Is the school delivering a fully comprehensive training?

Q Does the school train holistically?

In other words does the school 'look, listen and understand' the individual needs of the students or does it turn out students marching to the same drum!

I have sat on audition panels for many years and I

am aware that certain schools and colleges can be identified as turning out a particular type of student who wears the school's brand name and doesn't have his or her own individual identity.

Q Are you happy and comfortable with the location of the school?

Remember, this might be the first time you have lived away from home. Your new school or college will be your home for several years; and you need to make certain that the environment is such that you feel you would be happy and content.

Short courses

A number of drama schools run short Easter or summer courses. If you have a found a school that you particularly like, it might be worth taking one of these, to give you an idea of the training and help you to know that you have made the right choice.

Private visits

You may also be able to arrange a private visit to the drama school of your choice before you make your final decision.

➡️ **You are about to invest up to three years or possibly even four years of your life in your training so it is of vital importance that you make the right decision at this point.**

3   STARTING TO PREPARE FOR YOUR AUDITION

Once you have chosen your preferred school it is time to think how you are going to get a place and how your course will be funded.

It would be wise to audition for more than one school in order to give yourself as many wide-ranging options as possible. This will also give you the opportunity to gain audition experience.

You will need to take some time in preparing for your audition, making sure that you have gathered the right material to show your best qualities.   It is important to note that some schools are prescriptive about the choice of material presented at auditions while others leave it up to you to make the choice.

If you are hoping for a musical theatre course then you will probably be asked to present a song and a speech. You will be expected to show that you have a facility for movement and dance and the audition or examining panel will determine your physical capabilities during the audition.

If you want to become a triple threat performer you need to look at the different pathways and the various elements of the three disciplines of acting, singing and dance.

You need to look at all of these carefully, evaluate and then identify the right style for you to pursue and work on for your audition day.

Let us start with your song.

In order to give you some points of reference I have included names of lyricists and composers and original dates of productions so that you may begin to have an awareness of the chronology of musicals.

4   CHOOSING SUITABLE SONGS

Q Are you going to sing "I Dreamed A Dream" or "Stars" from the musical *Les Misérables* (Boublil & Schonberg, 1980) based on Victor Hugo's story, along with another third of the auditionees?

Q Are you going to surprise the panel with your knowledge of musical theatre and present an unheard of or little known and seldom heard song?

Do remember that once the panel has heard "I Dreamed A Dream" or "Stars" more than five times on a particular day, then your performance of it, unless totally brilliant and innovative, will probably go unnoticed.

However, if you walk in and announce that you are going to sing a little known song from an unknown musical or deliver a speech from an unusual or lesser-known play then you can be absolutely certain that the panel will appreciate that you have started to do your homework and have the capability to research.

It will be seen that you have an interest and curiosity towards the musical theatre repertoire; and this will prove that you have started to devour your passion and that you are serious about a professional career.

Researching a song

When you find a song from a musical that interests you, spend some time researching it:

- Find out about the composer and lyricist.

- Find out something about the singer who sang the song originally.

- Even find out who directed, choreographed or staged the original production.

You will find that these points of reference are an important part of your training; knowing who the choreographer was, for example, might reveal something about the particular style of work.

Later on, when you have begun your career you might be asked to dance in the style of Bob Fosse, Susan Stroman or Jerome Robbins or sing in the style of Ethel Merman, Howard Keel or Patti LuPone. As an actor you could be asked to perform in a melodramatic, farcical or Grand Guinol style.

When you start your research you will constantly come across the names of theatre innovators and exponents of theatre styles.

DO NOT be dismissive: it is more than likely that

these people were important contributors to the world of musical theatre historically and their legacy is probably still around today and to be found in many of the current musicals.

Finding your own style

Try and find your own way to present your song DON'T mimic the original performers. For example, a lot of people sing "Somewhere That's Green" from *Little Shop of Horrors* (Menken & Ashman, 1982) with a lisp in exactly the same way that Ellen Greene did originally – avoid aping an original idea.

Students can sometimes listen to a recording of the song they have chosen for an audition so often that they actually end up presenting a caricature of that particular performer!

Be unique – find a way of showing that your presentation and delivery isn't based on anyone else's.

Speeches leading into songs

Suddenly bursting into song after you have just

delivered your lines is the most unnatural thing that a performer is asked to do in the theatre. It is an art to naturally gear your speech into song and then back again into speech so that an audience is really unaware of the change of delivery.

Many good plays have been turned into musicals. You might find a speech that leads into a song suitable for use as part of your audition or examination package in one of these.

⇨ **You would do well to consider looking for something like this for your audition. This form of presentation is useful and effective.**

The suitability of material

It is important that you choose material that falls within your playing range with your song choices.

For example, there would be no point in a young person singing "Send In The Clowns" from *A Little Night Music* (Stephen Sondheim, 1973) or "Losing My Mind" from *Follies* (Stephen Sondheim, 1971). Songs like these are written for much older people and consequently won't always "speak" to you when you are young.

This means that you are going to have to spend some time researching i.e. looking for material that is appropriate, interesting and unusual by exploring the different types of songs that might or might not prove to be suitable for you.

For example, you might enjoy singing songs from the highly acclaimed stage musical *Chicago* (Kander and Ebb, 1975) or *Cabaret* (Kander and Ebb, 1966). Well, that is a terrific starting point for research. However, should you feel that Kander and Ebb songs suit your particular voice and style, seek out less well-known musicals written by the same team (there are lots!).

Kander and Ebb shows that have not attracted as much interest as *Chicago* and *Cabaret* (the ever popular, frequently staged musicals that have both been produced as blockbuster movies) include *Flora, The Red Menace* (1965), *The Happy Time* (1968) and *Steel Pier* (1997). All of these less well-known musicals contain wonderful songs that aren't constantly churned out at auditions.

If you look further than the handful of frequently staged popular musicals for material you should discover a little-performed gem of a song that will suit you perfectly for auditions or grade examinations.

You should be able to 'wear' a song or a speech in almost the same way that you wear clothes. It has to fit your body comfortably, add to your personality and enhance your presentation.

Presentation of a song

Remember, once the music starts so does your presentation of the song:

- The song might have a long introduction and it is your job to fill that introduction emotionally.

You can't just stand there and wait until the lyrics begin and it is your turn to start!

- The song doesn't end until the last note of music has faded away.

Your presentation of the song finishes when the last note of music has faded away. DON'T 'switch-off' immediately you have sung the final note.

- Don't be rushed into starting.

Tell the pianist that you will give a nod when you are ready.

This gives you some time to prepare and also time to get into character. It also shows the panel that you are in control of your presentation and audition.

The choice of songs available

* Ballad * Up-tempo * Patter * Torch and Anthem *
* Comedy * Point Number * Rock * Pop * Operetta *
* Classical * Belt * Character * Pastiche * Parlour *
* Blues * Song and Dance * Music-Hall *

⇨ In order to give yourself and the panel interesting choices, try to look at as many of the different types and styles of songs that are available. Then, decide which style would suit you best for your audition from that range.

It is almost certain that you will need to increase your vocabulary and understanding of the various song styles. If you research thoroughly you will then begin the fascinating journey of understanding the history of the musical.

It is important to note that the following examples given here in TYPES AND STYLES OF SONG (see p.36) are all very popular and will probably be used by someone else on the day of your audition!

It is up to you to find something original!

Discarded material

Composers frequently write material for shows that is subsequently discarded and this provides a useful source of little-known songs.

A good example is "Being Alive" the great climactic song from *Company* (Stephen Sondheim, 1970). Sondheim actually wrote two versions of the same song that he wasn't happy with prior to this – "Marry Me A Little" and "Multitudes Of Amy's". Both these discarded songs are equally good and, though they are published, seldom heard.

When Irving Berlin died, at the age of 102, a whole trunkful of unpublished songs was found among his possessions.

Indeed, his great anthem to the theatre "There's No Business Like Show Business" from *Annie Get Your Gun* (1946) was retrieved from a waste bin after he had discarded it, insisting that it was not very good!

Most musical theatre composers have heaps of 'cut' songs or 'trunk' songs. You will find songs like these both on recordings and in sheet music form and they are certainly worth discovering if you particularly enjoy a composer's known work.

NOTE: If a song has NOT been published it is a usual and accepted practise to ask an accomplished musician to transcribe from a recording.

BALLAD

A ballad is a popular song that has a romantic or sentimental theme. Hundreds of these slow songs have been written for musicals; so you will come up with something original if you search.

A ballad is traditionally a narrative poem or song (most often of folk origin). It consists of simple stanzas and usually has a refrain.

The ballad was used as an early form of "music in the theatre" (NOT "musical theatre" as we know it today) and these stage shows were known as **ballad operas**. The most famous of which is *The Beggar's Opera* written by John Gay in 1728.

This was reworked by Brecht in 1928 with Kurt Weill as his musical collaborator and re-titled *The Threepenny Opera (Die Dreigroschenoper),* and then reworked again in 1946 by Duke Ellington and called *The Beggar's Holiday.*

"Someone To Watch Over Me" from *Oh! Kay* (George and Ira Gershwin, 1926) is a perfect example of a ballad. This is a great standard and most of the well-known singers will have performed it on numerous occasions and you can almost guarantee that "Someone To Watch Over Me" will be chosen by someone else who is auditioning on the same day as you! Therefore, it is probably NOT a good idea to consider this for your audition.

➪ **Let's be unique**.

For example, you like the music of George Gershwin and you understand the lyrics of Ira Gershwin (Ira was George's brother and NOT his sister as many students wrongly assume, when asked); so explore their unknown and unsung works and you will be surprised what you find!

Up-tempo songs are usually high-energy songs. A typical example would be "Tonight At Eight" from *She Loves Me* (Bock and Harnick, 1963).

High-energy songs can be useful if you are nervous, because the amount of adrenalin that is needed to perform them means that you don't have time to allow your nerves to kick in and take control of your body. Also, if you are performing an up-tempo song you probably need to move with energy and this stops the feeling that you are rooted to the spot.

'Nerves are very hard to control – if one leg starts to shake then you can be sure the other leg will follow suit. . . . . . Then the tension creeps up to the hands and in trying to control those you start making fatuous gestures. . . . . . Unfortunately it doesn't end there, the symptoms of nervousness continue creeping upwards and will probably hit your voice just at the moment when you are going to sing a top C!' *

 * Refer to the Effective Communication handbook.

NOTE: The audition panel or examiner will understand that you are nervous and take it into consideration.

The more confident and prepared with your material you are, the less you need to worry.

PATTER

A patter song has an extraordinary number of tongue twisting lyrics that are usually sung very quickly.

A good example would be "I Am The Very Model Of A Modern Major General" from *The Pirates of Penzance* (Gilbert and Sullivan, 1879) or "Ya Got Trouble" from *The Music Man* (Meredith Wilson, 1957).

There are hundreds of good patter numbers with great titles like "How Could You Believe Me When I Said I Loved You When You Know I've Been A Liar All My Life" from the film *Royal Wedding* (Lane and Lemer, 1951). A more up-to-date example would be "Words, Words, Words" from *The Witches of Eastwick* (Dempsey and Rowe, 2000).

Patter songs are tricky pieces but they may be something you feel that you can do well and therefore might be worth exploring.

It is most important with songs of this type that your diction and clarity is absolutely first rate.

The panel may not get a sense of what you are singing if you swallow your words!

TORCH AND ANTHEMIC

A torch song is a big sing. It is usually about unrequited love and it is called a torch song because if someone is 'carrying a torch' for you it means that he or she is devoted to, or totally in love with you but that you don't feel the same way.

A good example of a torch song is "The Man That Got Away" from the film musical *A Star Is Born* (Harold Arlen and Ira Gershwin, 1955). "On My Own" from *Les Misérables* is another good example – but again both these songs are frequent visitors to the audition studio and are probably best avoided because of that!

Anthemic songs are similar to torch songs. We all know these rousing anthems – "Bui Doi" from *Miss Saigon* (Boublil and Schonberg, 1989) and "Anthem" from *Chess* (Andersson, Ulvaeus and Rice, 1986).

Anthemic songs can be very impressive if you have the sort of voice that is capable of a big sing.

However, it is vital that you check out the vocal range on the music copy and make sure that your voice has good strong sounds on <u>all</u> the notes if you intend singing an anthemic number.

COMEDY

You will find comedy songs in most musicals – and some of these songs have lyrics that are <u>so</u> pertinent to the musical that it is difficult to lift them from it. However, there are others that can work well.

<u>If comedy is your particular forte then you should start with the lyrics and not the music.</u>

Have a look at the lyrics of Lorenz Hart who was Richard Rodgers's partner for many years, writing such comedy songs as "To Keep My Love Alive" (*A Connecticut Yankee,* Rodgers and Hart, 1927).

You could look at the very witty and sometimes sophisticated comedy songs by Noel Coward who was the master of this genre. He wrote revue songs such as "Don't Put Your Daughter On The Stage, Mrs Worthington" and "Mad Dogs And Englishmen".

You might also listen to Tom Lehrer singing his own sardonic songs like "Poisoning Pigeons In The Park" or "I Hold Your Hand In Mine".

"I C'aint Say No" from *Oklahoma* (Rodgers and Hammerstein, 1943) is one of the most popular comedy songs and it turns up at nearly every audition! Therefore it is probably NOT a good choice.

I'm not suggesting that you should choose comedy songs for auditions unless you know that comedy is a strong point.

However, taking a look at songs with lyrics by Hart, Coward and Lehrer will, at the very least, help you to understand and identify the varied styles of comedy songs that are available.

It is also possible that songs like these might come in handy at a later date.

POINT NUMBER

When singing any song it is your job to communicate a sense of the lyrics to your audience or to the audition or examining panel.

Some songs need a heightened accentuation on particular words that will 'point' them out as being vital to the sense of the song.

With a good point number, the lyricist will have chosen a particular word for its fun, meaning or rhyming values. When the word is placed in the song and pointed out to the audience by you, it will release the comedy contained in the remainder of the song.

A good example of a point number like this would be "Invocation To The Gods" from *The Frogs* (Stephen Sondheim, 1974).

This doesn't mean that you can ignore pointing out lyrics in other styles of song (you will find any words that need pointing out if you explore the sense and stanza).

For example in the song "I Get A Kick Out Of you" from *Anything Goes* (Cole Porter, 1934) there are words that need to be pointed out by the performer "FLYing too HIGH in the SKY with some GUY is my Idea of nothing to do."

This style of lyric writing employed by Porter is quintessentially sophisticated and unlike the early 'rhyming' songs written at the time musical theatre was invented.

It is interesting to note that these rhyming songs of the early musical comedy period were often referred to as "Moon and June and Spoon" songs because the rhyming methods used were so very basic and naive.

There are good lyrics to be found in every type and style of song. You will need to work out how you are going to point or communicate these in order to release the sense of fun, wit and style of the song.

ROCK

Since the advent of rock musicals, which in turn became known as rock operas in the 1960's, rock songs have become part of the musical theatre industry.

A good example of a classic musical theatre rock song would be "Heaven On Their Minds" from *Jesus Christ, Superstar* (Andrew Lloyd Webber and Tim Rice, 1971).

There are courses available to students that are geared for 'modern' sounds and voices. If you are interested in this type of course, a rock song for your audition might prove to be an asset.

If you intend performing a rock number at auditions your rock choice doesn't necessarily have to come from the musical theatre repertoire, so you are provided with an extremely wide range of songs to look at and choose from.

Together with the rock operas and rock musicals there are musicals that deal with the 'rock and roll' era of the 50s and 60s.

Stage musicals such as the hugely popular 1970s *Grease* (Jacobs and Casey, 1972) – and equally successful 1978 film and *A Slice of Saturday Night* (The Heather Brothers, 1990) had original scores but there are musicals that do not.

For example the stage musical Buddy (1989) is loosely based on the life of the American pop idol Buddy Holly and uses the music that he made famous.

The more recent stage musical *We Will Rock You* (2002) features music from the rock band 'Queen' and lyrics with a thin fantasy storyline written by Ben Elton. The musical numbers are central to this musical and the plot does little more than link the numbers.

OPERETTA

Operetta! There is so much to say about this subject because operetta was one of the forerunners of today's musical.

Indeed, if you think about shows like *Phantom Of The Opera* (Lloyd Webber, Stilgoe and Hart, 1986) and *Les Misérables,* and you understand the work of the early operetta composers, you will see how the composers of operetta have influenced the composers of musicals today.

There are so many different styles of operetta – French, German, Viennese and the light or comic operas of England of course; that any study would fill many books (and has) exploring this one vast subject.

The works of Gilbert and Sullivan provide fine examples of the English light or comic opera, with operettas like *Trial by Jury* (1875) and *The Mikado* (1885).

Operetta burst forth with Lehar's *The Merry Widow* in 1905. Although operetta had started to change its form by the time the 1920s arrived, its influence remained and is still of great importance today.

Even Ivor Novello, who is acknowledged to be

Britain's leading composer of stage musicals between the two World Wars was actually writing in operatic style for the spectacular shows that were produced in London at the Theatre Royal, Drury Lane in the late 1930s through until his death in the early 1950s.

Noël Coward's romantic musical *Bitter-Sweet* written in the late 1920s was really an operetta rather than a musical, too.

So, if you think that you can sing songs like "Wishing I Were Somehow Here Again" from *Phantom of the Opera* or "A Heartful Of Love" from *Les Misérables* look at the operatic repertoire and you will discover some little-known gems that are equally good.

Take a look at the work of Sigmund Romberg, Rudolf Friml and Victor Herbert and you will find a wealth of material encompassing many different styles – from great lush ballads to comedy songs, providing a rich source of interesting and varied choices for your consideration.

CLASSICAL

If you have had singing lessons and have discovered that you have a classical voice, then you can present something from the classical repertoire. Although I would suspect that, with this choice, you might want to specialise in a classical training.

However, if musical theatre is what you want and you have the voice to sing songs from the classical repertoire, look at the work of the composers I've mentioned in the OPERETTA section (see p.47).

Songs like Coward's "I'll See You Again" from *Bitter-Sweet* (1929) or Novello's "Waltz of my Heart" from *The Dancing Years* (1939) can sound wonderful when sung with the classical voice.

BELT

Some people have a natural belt voice – although singers like these are very few and far between.

Unfortunately, quite often, a potential student will use their belt voice at an audition before it is ready.

There is bound to be a singing tutor on the panel who is likely to get quite alarmed if the belt voice is not being used properly.

You must be prepared for singing tutors to look closely to see if you have done any damage to your vocal chords if they are worried.

Belt singing is a very particular way of using your voice.

Unless you have a natural belt voice, it is imperative to make sure that your 'belt' is properly trained. If not, you could do irreparable damage to your vocal chords and possibly lose your career.

This is the reason why many singing tutors will coach their students to a stage that falls short of allowing them to sing in belt, until they know that they are absolutely ready.

One of the greatest examples of an exponent of belt

singing was the Broadway star Ethel Merman who claimed that she had never had a singing lesson in her life.

I don't want to get too academic at this point but I will explain a little about belt singing and then you have to decide whether you have a belt voice or not.

Belt singing is a style or technique of singing in which the larynx is slightly higher than in the classical voice, and the vocal cords are held tightly together for longer periods of time. The shape of the word and how it is spoken is intrinsic to the sound. The space inside the mouth, in both the classical technique and the belt, is neither a chest voice nor an extension of chest voice into the higher register.

Q Confused?

Don't panic! Singing tutors at drama school are all aware of the nature of belt singing and they will guide you through the technicalities of how to make it work for you – but only when you are ready to embrace it.

A lot of people think that singing belt means singing loudly and energetically. This is NOT so. Be wise about singing this particular style and get advice before you embark on ruining the major tool of your trade.

To give you an idea of a good belt song look at "Some People" from *Gypsy* (Jule Styne, 1959) with lyrics by Stephen Sondheim.

Better still listen the greatest belter of them all, Ethel Merman singing Irving Berlin's "There's No Business Like Show Business".

CHARACTER

I suppose it could be argued that all songs from musicals are character songs; because they are all sung by a particular character in the show.

In musical theatre terms 'character' songs are usually performed by a second lead or featured player and serve as a continuation of the story, a divertissement or a vignette (a character sketch). And these songs often tell their own story about the character.

Character songs are often amusing or extremely funny and many are held in a great deal of affection. Quite often, and particularly in the case of a good revival, a character song becomes the high spot of the show that we all look forward to when we go to see the musical.

"Adelaide's Lament" from *Guys and Dolls* (Frank Loesser, 1950) is one of the great character songs from a musical, and also "I'm Just A Girl Who Can't Say No" from Rodgers and Hammerstein's *Oklahoma* (1943).

More modern examples of great character songs include "Master of the House" from *Les Misérables* and "Mister Cellophane" from *Chicago.*

Not only does the song "Master of the House" tell you

a lot about the character of Thenardier but it also contains information that is important to the musical as a whole. Yet the song is almost self-contained – almost like a one act play.

"Mister Cellophane" brilliantly describes the character of Amos precisely in one song. Yet this song works equally well taken from the show, out of context.

PASTICHE

Pastiche means to take an affectionate look at a period, style or even a person. Lots of musicals have been written as a pastiche.

Sandy Wilson's *The Boyfriend* (1954) is a prime example of a pastiche musical comedy. Taking inspiration from several early shows of the 1920s – and in particular *No No Nanette* (Youmans, Ceaser and Harbach, 1925) Wilson created a musical that was a loving re-creation of a particular period and style.

The 1933 film *42nd Street* (Harry Warren and Al Dubin) was used as the idea for the 1968 pastiche musical *Dames At Sea* (Wise, Haimsohn and Miller). *42nd Street* (a putting-on-a-show musical in which the leading lady is indisposed and a chorus girl is told to get out there and come back a star) finally arrived as a stage musical in 1980 – 47 years after its premiere in the cinema!

Neither *The Boyfriend* nor *42nd Street* 'send up' or caricature the featured period. Both these musicals are a genuine recreation of a style of music, lyrics, story and even design, which combine to create a new look from an old theme.

Even the 1970s stage musical *Grease* is a pastiche

because it takes an affectionate look back at 1950s American teenagers and college days without being unfaithful.

Warren Casey and Jim Jacobs's endearing pastiche songs like "Its Raining On Prom Night", "Beauty School Dropout" and "There Are Worse Things I Could Do" have become classics of the musical theatre stage.

NOTE: Pastiche is not to be confused with caricature!

Pastiche imitates and is faithful to the original period in every way.

Caricature is a grotesque and usually comic representation of characters by the exaggeration of characteristic traits.

PARLOUR

This is a really unusual category, but one worth exploring if we are to take an overall look at song styles.

Parlour songs were made popular by the American composer Stephen Foster and are exactly what the name suggests. They were written for families – to entertain themselves by gathering around a piano for an informal singsong in the parlour long before television and radio were ever thought of.

Foster was a master of popular parlour songs like "I Dreamed Of Jeannie With The Light Brown Hair" and "Just A Song At Twilight". Although these songs were never intended for the musical stage they did turn up in several musical films; including a couple of films that were 'biopics' i.e. biographical films about Stephen Foster.

There are some wonderful finds awaiting discovery among songs of this type. I can guarantee, that if you find a parlour song you like, you will be the only person on the day of your audition performing it!

Good news for the audition panel.

The word 'blue' has been associated with melancholia or depression for hundreds of years so it comes as no surprise to find "blues" songs in musicals.

When African and European music first merged, slaves sang songs filled with words speaking of their extreme suffering and desperation and a style of music began to evolve that eventually became known as the blues.

However, even though the concept of the blues has grown out of great pain and although the dramatic telling of blues songs is usually about heartache and sorrow, blues songs aren't exclusively mournful. There was, and is, pathos to be found in blues music but also humour that pushes the human condition into another area of play.

Musical theatre had a field day when the blues started to infiltrate musicals, and both humorous and sad "blues" style songs were written for a wide variety of shows.

For example, the first line of "Buddy's Blues" from *Follies* "I've got those God-why-don't-you-love-me-oh-you-do-I'll-see-you-later-Blues", immediately tells us that we are listening to a blues song that is a masterpiece of patter and comedy, and that it is up-tempo and has dramatic intensity. Another wonderful comedy blues number is "The Red Blues" from *Silk Stockings* (Cole Porter, 1955) – and this is about communism!

There have also been many compilation musicals celebrating the blues such as *Blues In The Night, Jelly's Last Jam* and *Black and Blue* that contain both serious and funny blues songs.

Shows featuring blues songs are well worth exploring.

You will turn up good audition songs – even serious blues numbers like "Where Has My Hubby Gone Blues" from *No, No Nanette* are seldom used at auditions.

SONG AND DANCE

If you have dance or movement skills it may be that you want to show these during your song so that the panel can see that you are well on the way to becoming a triple threat performer.

There are numerous songs that have this facility. They usually contain a dance break for you to perform your movement before returning to the last bars of the song.

A lot of male performers use the song and dance number "All I Need Is The Girl" from *Gypsy* at auditions. This is a great song – but unfortunately it is done to death! And the female most popular choice is "I Can Do That" from *Chicago*.

However, if you look among the hundreds of musicals spanning the years, for something different for your audition, you will find a suitable song and dance number that can be brought fresh and new to the panel in practically every one.

➪ **Remember, if you are going to dance or move make sure that you have thought out your choreography or routine and that it is as finely rehearsed as your song. DON'T leave the movement to chance.**

MUSIC-HALL

Music-hall is a very British entertainment. It is now often referred to nostalgically as 'old tyme music-hall'.

There are all sorts of songs that make up the music-hall repertoire: up-tempo, ballads, comedy, etc. "Any Old Iron" is an example of an up-tempo patter song. "The Boy I Love Is Up In The Gallery" is a good example of a ballad and "Which Switch Miss, Is The Switch Miss, For Ipswich?" is an example of a comedy song.

Some of the popular songs that came from the Victorian and Edwardian halls are as well known now as they ever were. You probably know songs like, "Daddy Wouldn't Buy Me A bow Wow", "Daisy bell" (A Bicycle Built For Two), "Love's Old Sweet Song" (Just A Song At Twilight), "The Man Who Broke The Bank At Monte Carlo", "Waiting At The Church" and "Wot Cher!" (Knock'd 'Em In The Old Kent Road).

Music-hall songs are seldom used for auditions. Therefore, these songs are worth consideration – take the time to search for good songs.

You might find useful audition material that is both interesting and unusual.

6   ORIGINS OF SONGS AND STAGE MUSICALS

Tracing the history of songs and musicals by looking at the development of the original form of the work is a fascinating hobby in itself – starting with the source material and following the subsequent changes and eventual transformation into a musical.

▷ **Try this as an exercise:**

Trace the evolution of the musical *Hello, Dolly!*

If you do, then I guarantee some surprises!

Researching source material will help you to study situation and enable you to think about character analysis. You will start to be aware that the ideas and styles of work of some of those early composers are still very much in existence in today's modern musicals.

The importance of this type of research cannot be overestimated.

Researching a song (see also p.28) and looking at it in context will not only enlighten your performance of that song but you will add a little more to your knowledge of theatre history at the same time.

Classical material

A number of the great classical composers have had their works adapted and turned into musicals.

Although George Forrest and Robert Wright were a composer and lyricist in their own right, producing their own original material, they established a reputation and achieved popularity by reworking the classics.

Forrest and Wright transformed Greig's music into *Song of Norway* (1944), Borodin's music into *Kismet* (1953), and Rachmaninov's into *Anya* (1965) – based on the story of the Russian princess, Anastasia.

Perhaps the greatest transformation from the opera stage to the musical stage was the reworking of George Bizet's opera *Carmen.* The original opera was written in 1875 and turned into the Americanised *Carmen Jones* by Oscar Hammerstein in 1943 by cleverly reworking and reconstructing Bizet's music into musical theatre form.

Some of the great opera stories have even found their way into musicals with new and original scores.

For example, Giacomo Puccini's *Madame Butterfly* (1904) and *La Bohème* (1896) became *Miss Saigon* and *Rent* (Jonathon Larson, 1996). The Guiseppe

Verdi opera *Aida,* written in 1871, is now a worldwide hit as the Elton John and Tim Rice musical *Aida* (2000).

The works of Shakespeare

Shakespeare's plays have also been used as a source of inspiration for the musical stage. We all know that Shakespeare's play *Romeo and Juliet* was the source for the stage musical *West Side Story* (Bernstein and Sondheim, 1957) and film (1961), and *The Taming of the Shrew* was the inspiration for Cole Porter's *Kiss Me Kate* before that in 1948.

There are many other examples such as *Othello,* which inspired the 1968 rock musical *Catch My Soul* (Pohlman, Zoghby and Good) and *Twelfth Night* which became *Your Own Thing* (Apolinar and Hester, 1968).

More recent productions include another stab at *Twelfth Night* called *Play On* (1997) using the music of Duke Ellington as its source. *The Taming of the Shrew* has also been seen again as a new production called *Romancin' The One I Love* (Briggs and West, 2000) and there is even another *Romeo and Juliet* (Presgurvic and Black, 2002).

NOTE: Composers of musicals are continually looking at the works of the great dramatist Shakespeare because his plays have great potential as works for the musical theatre.

Screen musicals

One of the current trends is to take musicals that were originally written for the screen and rework them for the stage.

Saturday Night Fever (The Bee Gees, 1977) and *Footloose* (Snow and Pitchford, 1984) started out as cinema films, but owing to their popularity, were turned into stage musicals. These musicals were both staged in 1998 for the first time and were received with great critical acclaim and found new audiences.

However, adapting screen musicals for the stage is not a new idea.

Meet Me In St. Louis (Martin and Blane, 1944), *State Fair* (Rogers & Hammerstein, 1945), *Singing In The Rain* (Brown and Freed, 1952) and *Chitty Chitty Bang Bang* (Richard and Robert Sherman, 1968) all started out as film musicals in the 1940s and

1950s and were thought worthy enough to adapt for the stage.

There are many more examples to be found of screen musicals like these that have subsequently proved successful as stage musicals.

7   PREPARING YOUR AUDITION MATERIAL

It is essential that you prepare your audition material carefully.

At last you have found several songs that you feel might be suitable for your audition.

➢ You have learnt the words and researched the background to the songs of your choice.

➢ You have decided whether you are going to sing each song as it was originally intended in the musical from which it came or if you are going to sing it out of context.

➢ And finally you've decided on the performance values that you are going to give the songs.

The next steps

Next, you have to take that whole package a couple of steps further.

• Record your singing voice so you can listen to the sounds that you are making.

• Perform your songs in front of a mirror to observe your body language.

67

DON'T ever pick up a song or speech without looking at the wider picture. Always read the whole libretto or play. You need to understand why the song or speech is there and have a good clear understanding of what the lyricist or playwright intended.

This research will also throw some light on why the character sings the song or makes the speech and the mood s/he is in when it is delivered.

Find a song that sits comfortably within your vocal range. For example, you might have a reasonable belt voice but a weak head voice – and if the song requires both it is quite likely that one element will let you down.

You may have an acting or singing coach – ask him/her to go through your choices and rehearse you until you are both totally confident that you have explored the lyrics and the emotional truth of any song to its limit.

It is imperative that you present with clarity and with understanding, and that you demonstrate an intelligent approach to the interpretation of the lyrics.

The elements of your voice

Explore ways by which you are going to take the panel or the examiner on the journey of the song with you.

Q How are you going to use the different elements of your voice to excite and thrill?

If you sing the song on one emotional level, without any colouring or tone, it will appear bland and dull.

Look at the music very carefully and you will notice that most of the work has been done for you by the composer and lyricist.

All you have to do is make the song live.

Look to see if there is a key change in the music or if there is a particularly lyric that brings the song together. You will need to work vocally and emotionally towards this high point to create the magical moment in the song that will electrify your audience.

Breathing and phrasing

Now is the time to think about your breathing techniques. If you take a breath in the wrong place it can alter the sense of the song.

Think about your phrasing – one of the great musical theatre stars who is sublimely expert on phrasing and breathing is Barbara Cook. Listen to her recordings in order to understand that phrasing is an art in itself, or listen to Frank Sinatra who was another master of phrasing.

Better still listen to the work of both these great artists.

Gestures

Any gestures that you make while presenting a song should come from within and not be planned.

The term 'coming from within' means that you have 'inhabited a character', either the character that is explained in the libretto or one that you have invented.

If you have totally immersed yourself in the character and you understand the 'feelings' in the song then any gesture you might make will appear to be natural and not premeditated and contrived.

Accents

You will need to make some choices about the accent you use.

A lot of the popular songs used for musical auditions are taken from American musicals. If you sing these with the appropriate accent you will find that the lyrics work. However, if you don't apply the accent, it can sometimes become very difficult to make certain words rhyme and the lyrics simply don't work.

DON'T even consider using an accent unless you have done considerable work on it and the accent is effective.

If you are not confident you might feel that it would be a safer option to stick to neutral ground and rely instead on songs that do NOT require an accent.

Songs taken out of context

It may be that you decide to take a song out of context and present it in a different or unusual way. If you take a song out of context you must carefully think through the choices you make as to how you are going to present your work.

It is perfectly acceptable to take a song out of context but DON'T expect panel members or examiners to be mind readers.

You must be prepared to explain how you have arrived at the decisions you have made.

This will provide you with the opportunity to let the panel or your examiner see how well prepared you are and show your ability to take control of the situation.

Compilation books

There are many compilation music books available containing all the 'popular' hits. However, there are good reasons why you should NOT use books like these; but if you do intend using one of them at least search out the original libretto.

Compilation books usually set the music in a different key from the original score – a 'songs made easy' copy. The key signatures are sometimes lowered in order that the songs are accessible for most voices.

The original key signatures are usually much brighter than those found in compilation books.

You would be far better off finding the original score in a library or obtaining a copy of it from the music publisher.

Props

You may want to use props – and this is acceptable. However, there are certain props that arrive at auditions that give the song away before you have even announced it!

For example, if someone walks in with a book in their hand then you can be sure that this candidate is going to sing "Adelaide's Lament" from *Guys and Dolls* or if someone gets out a pad and a pencil then it's sure to be "Dear Friend" from *She Loves Me* and a newspaper tells the panel that the song will be "Crossword Puzzle" from *Starting Here, Starting Now* (Maltby and Shire, 1977).

These are all wonderful songs – but they are very popular audition choices. Should you choose to sing one of these songs at an audition it is highly likely that you will NOT be the only person. Therefore, you would probably do better to find more unusual material.

Sheet music

In the profession the music copy is usually referred to as 'the dots'.

Once you feel satisfied that you have collected a suitable selection of songs for your audition, make sure that you put the sheet music neatly into a file, so the musical director can read the music clearly and also be able to turn pages with ease.

<u>You must ensure that any sheet music that is required for the audition is neat and clearly marked-up.</u>

DO'S:

- Mark your music with any changes that you want the pianist to follow.

- Make sure that you set the tempo that you require.

- Ask for a bell note if you are worried about pitching your voice.

- Ask the pianist to follow you if you want to take the lead.

- If you forget your words simply ask the pianist if

you can start the song again or pick it up from where you dried. <u>This will make no difference to your getting a place or not.</u>

- Instruct your accompanist if there is anything particular that you do in your presentation that is of relevance. For example, you might want to hold a note longer than suggested or have the pianist follow you in certain free passages.

DON'T'S:

- DON'T forget to mark any changes to the music that you decide to make on your music copy.

- DON'T take a crumpled piece of music to the audition.

- DON'T sellotape a lot of pages together so that the music hardly fits on the piano stand.

- DON'T present the pianist with a sheaf of loose pages because they will probably end up on the floor!

- Should you forget your words and dry DON'T let it destroy you – it WON'T go against you.

Time yourself – a song lasting NO longer than two minutes is required for an audition.

Therefore it is important that you take the length of a song into consideration when making your choices.

If you find a song you like that is longer than the required length you might decide to cut it – this is perfectly acceptable.

However, if you do, you must make sure that the cut version still contains enough information for you to be able to "tell the story".

Do I need an accompanist?

Yes. You will need an accompanist.

- DON'T sing unaccompanied.

- DON'T take a backing track.

DON'T consider singing unaccompanied or singing to a backing track at your audition unless it is specified by the drama school or the syllabus; for the simple reason that neither enables an audition panel to assess your musicality with much clarity.

The Musical Director

Give yourself time to talk to the musical director about the tempo and point out any changes that are marked on the music in order that s/he is able to accompany you well.

If you are worried about pitching your voice ask for a bell note before you start. This will indicate the note that is needed for you to start the song (you then hold it in your head until you begin).

If the tempo isn't right when you start the song have the confidence to stop the audition and ask if you can spend a few moments with the musical director in order to get it right.

Always use the correct terms when you instruct the musical director. For example, if you want the musical director to follow you then you should ask him/her to accompany you 'colla voce' which means that you take the lead and the pianist will follow you.

Adopt a professional manner when you are instructing the musical director. Then the panel will acknowledge your knowledge of music and admire your professionalism, appreciating that you are totally confident in taking control of your audition.

We have looked at the criteria for exploring and presenting songs (see p.27) and <u>most</u> of the same criteria can be applied to your acting audition.

 Before we look at the different acting styles that you might like to study, let us review the basic elements that combine to make a good acting piece. You will also find a great deal of help with this in the other handbooks in this series.

> ➢ Research your character thoroughly by reading the whole play and getting an idea of the playwright's style by looking at other plays s/he has written.

DON'T just read the speech printed out on a sheet – always go away and find the play and read the whole thing.

> ➢ Acquaint yourself with the style and period of the piece.

> ➢ Try to imagine what the character might be wearing and how you would physically be able to move in clothing of that type.

For example, you might be doing a speech from *The Importance of being Earnest.* If you are female try to imagine what it would be like to be corseted and laced and wearing a dress that sweeps the floor, or if you are a male what it might feel like to wear a stiff collar and a morning suit.

You should try sitting, standing and moving about in constrictive garments.

You might want to hire a costume to give you a complete understanding of the feel of a style of dress – this will certainly change your body language and add to your performance.

➢ Think about the social manners and behaviour conveyed by your character.

I'm sure that the characters in the 1895 Oscar Wilde play *The Importance of being Earnest* would drink from a teacup and eat cucumber sandwiches totally differently from how we do today.

➢ Make sure that you find something that is within your playing range.

➢ Think about your diction, clarity and projection.

➢ Think about your breathing, phrasing and vocal range.

- Get used to sight-reading.

Read aloud at home and get used to speaking with good diction and work on your clarity, as well as looking at, and understanding, the deeper meaning of the text, in order that the speech isn't on a superficial level.

➡ Record your spoken voice and listen to the sounds that you are making. (This also applies to the singing voice see p.67.)

Q Are the sounds acceptable?

- Perform your speeches in front of a mirror to observe your body language. (This also applies to your songs see p.67.)

There are lots of books with titles like *"Audition Speeches for Actors".* These books are useful for introducing the young actor to different styles of theatre writing – and will often identify good monologues for auditions purposes.

At your audition

You might be asked to present a classical and a

modern speech at your audition. Therefore you must ensure that you are fully prepared to deliver both types of speech if you are called upon to do so.

It is also possible that the panel may feel you have made a wrong choice with your chosen piece and ask you if you have another speech. This happens sometimes.

Be prepared!

All candidates should present the panel or the examiner with a copy of their speech.

However, DON'T forget that the panel aren't interested in looking at what is written on your piece of paper because they are more interested in looking at you.

Be prepared to discuss your characterisation with the panel and why you made certain choices in your presentation.

If you forget your words, either during your speech or your song, DON'T let it destroy you. It happens a lot – and it also happens at professional auditions.

Simply ask the panel if you can start the speech again or pick it up where you dried.

If you 'dry' and many actors do, it means that you have temporarily forgotten your words and either need a cue or a moment of concentration in order to get back on track.

If you dry it WON'T go against you; it will make NO difference to your getting a place or not.

9   PREPARING FOR YOUR DANCE AUDITION

Many of the students who audition for musical theatre courses have never really taken dance as a serious discipline.

Because of this, auditionees who are worried and frightened by this aspect of the audition process can often be seen hanging about nervously at the back of the studio hardly wishing to partake.

This immediately sorts out those that can, those that can't and those that want to try.

Professional dance training can be divided into four categories:

> ballet
> contemporary
> musical theatre (jazz) dance
> tap

It may well be that you have some experience of all of these.

However, if dance is something that you have never embraced before, it would be very worthwhile starting dancing classes locally in order that you have some idea of how to manipulate and move your body.

When you attend dancing classes you will become

familiar with the basic terms that might be used at your audition by the dance tutor such as 'step-ball-change' or 'pirouettes' (turns). In addition, you will gain a knowledge of dance that will help you to understand how choreographers join step sequences and movements together to create a routine. You will also start to train your memory by memorising dance step sequences.

Memory training

Obviously, you need to memorise the dance steps in order to execute the routine well at your audition.

Memory and the ability to memorise is an extremely important part of the training at drama school.

You must train your mind to receive and retain information – whether it is from a script or directions from a director or choreographer.

You need to understand how to process that information and you need to know about the parts of your body that are going to transmit and execute this information – the process of understanding how to do this is called 'muscle memory'.

The dance tutor

Try not to cover your body up at your dance audition – otherwise the dance tutor and the others on panel won't be able to observe your physicality or see how you use your body. You need to think carefully about what you are going to wear and choose suitable clothing (see Dress do's and don'ts p.86).

Be prepared for a dance tutor to touch your body – s/he will be looking for any problems that you might have or feeling where you are placing certain muscles.

- If you have a problem or phobia about being touched it is important to explain this quietly to the tutor.

You will be given some warm-up exercises before you start. If you have had an injury or there is a particular part of your body that you have to protect make sure that you tell the dance tutor.

If the dance tutor knows that an exercise is probably going to be difficult for you because of injury, the panel will understand and you will not be asked to do that particular exercise.

- Get to know what your body is capable of – don't put it in danger.

10 THE DAY OF YOUR AUDITION

Make an effort to look neat and tidy on the day of your audition or examination.

Musical theatre performers have style and this comes partly from how they dress. To have an abundance of style is an important requirement for any musical theatre performer!

Dress dos and don'ts

Most drama schools will supply you with a list of items that the panel would like you to bring on the day of your audition.

If you look good and feel good about yourself then you are going to enhance the performance and the presentation of your pieces. You need to wear clothing that you feel comfortable in and have something to wear that is comfortable for your dance audition.

➢ It is advisable NOT to wear jewellery, a wristwatch or anything that might catch.

➢ It is particularly important NOT to wear jewellery in any piercings – although these are universally

➢ accepted as modern fashion accessories.

Body jewellery – can be dangerous when you suddenly stretch or leap, especially when you dance.

Tongue studs – can create an unwelcome distraction, especially if you are singing or delivering a speech.

Studs, hoops and chains – through ears, nose, mouth and eyebrows can create a distraction at the very least and are all potentially dangerous!

DON'T forget to remove all jewellery from piercings before the audition if you wear any.

I have auditioned more than one prospective student with a tongue piercing! On each occasion I became transfixed, marvelling at the medical technology that will allow someone to sing with an encumbrance, instead of listening to the song presentation!

One of the most remarkable features about you is your face and the panel will want to see it in order to observe how you are exploring the text when you deliver your speech, and how you express emotion when you sing and dance.

Do make sure that your hair is kept well off your face.

Feeling unwell

If you are feeling unwell at the time of your audition DON'T apologise to the panel.

If you have a cold or toothache or you are feeling unwell on the day of your audition you are not going to be able to give your best, and the panel will find it difficult to assess you.

The best thing to do is to telephone the drama school and re-arrange your audition if this is practicable.

Getting a place at drama school is difficult and you simply can't afford to audition on a wing and a prayer.

11 YOUR INTERVIEW

The audition panel is not there to catch you out and make you feel uncomfortable.

Members of the panel want to see what you are able to do and then make an informed judgement as to whether you have potential that can be developed for training in the three disciplines.

The panel might interview you as part of the audition process in order to determine how serious you are about training. They will want to find out why you want to be an actor and what sort of actor you would like to be.

You need to remember that the basis of being a triple threat performer is acting. Acting is a vital discipline, without it you won't be able to sing with intention or dance with conviction.

➢ The panel might want to discuss your favourite playwright, composer or lyricist with you.

➢ You might be asked about your favourite actor and what it is about him or her that impresses you.

➢ You will probably be asked how often you go to the theatre.

➤ You might be asked to give a critical appraisal of something you have seen recently.

➤ The panel might want to explore your pieces and why you chose them.

The panel will be assessing your knowledge and intent and determination to succeed and will want to see that you can talk about your experiences and ambitions.

The panel will expect you show an interest in and curiosity about the profession that you would like to be part of. You must be prepared to explain why you have chosen their particular drama school and it is also important that you arm yourself with questions that you would like to ask.

If the school runs a recall audition system the panel will probably sit down at the end of the day and decide who they would like to see again – and might ask you back for the second audition, a 'recall weekend'.

At the recall weekend you will work with tutors on acting techniques, singing classes and voice work.

The reason for this additional audition is twofold.

Firstly, it is to see whether you have any physical restraints that might get in the way of your career.

For example you might have incurred an injury that would make dance classes difficult for you or you might have a serious vocal problem. Usually, this will be pointed out to you, and it might be suggested that you take some time out in order to get your problems solved. On the other hand it is possible that the panel has seen enough talent in other areas and might consider structuring the course to suit your particular needs.

If you have any problems it is wise to let the drama school know before you audition.

Some auditionees are worried about mentioning physical problems but a good drama school will take these into consideration. For example, a lot of prospective students are worried if they have dyslexia – again, a good drama school will have a method in place to be able to deal with this.

If tutors are not made aware of your problems they will soon find out!

The second reason for recalling you is to find out how well you communicate and work as a member of a group.

Tutors will see if you understand your own contribution to the workshop and can work towards interpretation of a character. They need to know if you can concentrate in the face of many possible distractions and that you can confront difficulties and accept challenges.

Something else that might be noticed is that you are pulling focus away from the group towards yourself. The panel will also be finding out how well you understand the workings of your body and looking to see that you have a natural physical ability.

Remember, working in a play or a musical makes you an important member of a theatre company and the panel will want to see if you integrate well and will be observing how well you contribute to whatever you are asked to do.

You will need to prove that you can work successfully in a group situation without pulling focus and distracting others and show that you understand and value your own contribution to the workshop as well as contributions by others.

It is important to listen to the workshop leader as you

will be expected to carry out and interpret instructions with competency.

➪ There are three rules when someone is being asked to do something:

> Receive (information)
> Process (information)
> Execute (information)

Basically, this means listening carefully to the instructions given, organising those instructions in your head and then delivering them back to the leader or director in the way that has been instructed.

Once you have the ability to do this it will it will show that you have an active mind and that you can understand and carry out instructions. Receive, process and execute is particularly important in dance.

You may be asked to do something that you find quite challenging – you must be prepared to face any difficulty that this might present and respond to it. Actors are often asked by directors (in this case workshop leaders) to do something that they might never have done before. You must let the tutors see, not only that you are malleable, but also eager, to explore and experience new skills and new ideas.

For example, if you are asked to stand on your head the response should be 'well, I've never done it before but if you show me how I'll certainly have a go'!

Listen and react positively to new ideas, as this will demonstrate to the panel that you can put aside fear and anxiety and allow yourself to show awareness and trust.

Throughout your audition it is important to show truth in everything you do.

Truth in the song, truth in the speech and truth in dance.

The panel will be observing your attitude in your workshop, your ability to listen and your reaction to ideas. As long as you are well prepared and focussed you will be noticed.

What is the panel looking for?

Let us think about what the panel is going to be looking for.

First and foremost it is potential – members of the panel need to know that you have the ability to be trained in order to become a part of the industry. Remember, the school that you hope to attend is probably serving the industry and the 'new life' that goes into the heritage of the theatre is of vital important.

The panel will be observing how you present yourself and whether you have confidence in terms of determination, style, dress and manners. The panel will also be looking at how well you listen and whether you have a good attention span.

The panel will be interested in how you communicate and understand the words that you are singing or speaking and they will be listening to the 'sounds' that you are making with your spoken and singing voice.

The voice is one of the most important tools of the trade for this profession and the panel will be listening to its audible quality.

You might be asked to speak in R.P. This is 'received pronunciation' and is taught at most drama schools. Basically it means that you pronounce all the consonants – particularly those at the end of words and also that you have nice sounding vowel sounds.

Some students confuse speaking R.P. with speaking 'posh'. It is NOT – R.P. should lead you towards good clarity and clean speaking.

NOTE: It is the current fashion to speak what is called 'estuary' or 'lazy' English' a lazy drawl spoken almost from the back of the throat.

You might be asked to 'sight read' a piece of text at your audition.

This gives you an opportunity to show the panel that you have good reading skills, how you immediately understand and communicate the text, how you fill the space and how good your projection is.

Try not to become 'script bound' this means that when you are reading don't keep you eyes glued to the text without favouring front because if you do you will have lost your power to communicate.

There is little point in standing in front of a panel and reeling off a shopping list.

The accredited drama schools are very selective – they only want the best talent that is around in

any one particular year.

The competition for places is great, but if you have set your heart on drama training and you are one hundred per cent committed, and think that you have enough raw talent then you should go ahead.

Who's on the panel?

The panel will usually consist of members of the faculty along with people from the profession. They will be assessing you the moment you walk through the door.

Remember, this means that you need to have worked on your choices long before your audition day in order that you are totally secure and sure of the pieces that you are going to present.

Remember, if you have prepared your audition well and can show that you are a serious contender for a place then you will have shown the panel an idea of your commitment.

Remember, the panel will be aware that you are likely to be nervous on the day of your audition and this will taken into account.

You might not hear immediately if you have been offered a place or not.

The panel will spend a lot of time deliberating about each student. Remember, the drama school that you hope to attend is interviewing far more talented people than there are places available – the potential, aptitude, attitude and suitability of each candidate will be carefully assessed.

Suppose I'm not offered a place

Remember, you are auditioning the school . . . . . just as the school is auditioning you.

Thousands of people apply to drama schools each year and if you are not offered a place it doesn't mean that you have failed. It could be that the panel feels that you are not quite ready mentally and physically to take on such an enormous task or that the particular school isn't the right one for you.

If you are not offered a place and still determined to try for a career in the theatre, DON'T despair. Go away and think about how you presented

at the audition and start preparing to try again. Spend the next year working to gain additional experience and confidence – by training at your local drama club or studio, taking singing lessons and extending your work in dance.

Feedback

Generally, drama schools aren't in a position to give feedback.

Remember, a drama school will probably see between one thousand and two thousand applicants each year.

However, a good drama school will often tell you at interview level that you have potential and that it would be worth your while trying again the next year. The panel might advise you that you are not yet ready to take on such a demanding course, for example, or give you some indication as to what you need to work on in order to try again the following year.

If you are NOT given any feedback try to find out if it would be worth your auditioning again by contacting the drama school.

Remember, you can obtain helpful feedback if you enter for a Trinity examination.

Interview pitfalls

⇨ **Prepare and research – avoid interview pitfalls.**

If you are interviewed after your audition or examination the panel or examiner will be looking to see how interested and involved you are in the world of musical theatre; and will want to find out how well you have prepared and researched your pieces. The panel or examiner might want to discuss your characterisation of a role with you, for example, or ask why you chose a song by a particular composer!

I remember once auditioning a young lady who sang "Summertime" from the folk opera *Porgy and Bess* (George Gershwin, 1935). When I began the conversation at her interview I felt I was on safe ground by saying that I assumed she enjoyed singing the music of Gershwin. The young lady replied by saying that she had never heard of him!

On another occasion I asked a prospective student to name her favourite composer. She replied that it was definitely Cameron MacIntosh!

Needless to say, neither candidate was offered a place. They hadn't shown the first idea of possessing any knowledge whatsoever about the industry that they wanted to be part of; and they had obviously not even considered research.

Another student I auditioned presented the song "Look What Happened To Mabel" from *Mack And Mabel* (Michael Stewart and Jerry Herman, 1974) and I asked if she was singing it as the character Mabel. The student said that she was so I asked her to tell me a little about the character. "Oh! It's about some woman who works in some shop, becomes some film star and marries some film director." When I asked her to name the film star and film director she said she didn't know. Although she had no idea who wrote the musical I asked her to name the show. She told me, *Mack and Mabel,* so I asked if the title might throw some light on my previous question. I suggested this could lead her in the direction of a little research . . . . . but she said "no", she didn't think so, as it "didn't seem important." Needless to say she wasn't offered a place, either!

I often ask prospective students how they think 'musical theatre' started. I am given many different and interesting replies to this question. Anything from "Oh! It must have been Andrew Lloyd Webber who began it all." to "Cameron MacIntosh started it with *Les Misérables.*"

In order that this doesn't happen to you let us take a brief look at how the musical theatre started. Then it is up to you to fill in the gaps!

➪ **Remember, the preparation and research of your material is an important part of the process of getting a place.**

There has been music in the theatre since the time of the Ancient Greeks. In the Elizabethan age William Shakespeare used music in a number of his plays and he even described music as 'the food of love' in *Twelfth Night*; and we know that 17th century ballad operas employed music that was mostly 'folk' in style.

Then, much later . . . . . sometime, somewhere, someone came up with two of the most evocative and exciting words in the English language for lovers of musical theatre – MUSICAL COMEDY.

This all came about in 1866 when a theatre company in New York was presenting a new (and not very good!) melodrama called *The Black Crook.* At the same time an unlucky French ballet troupe, billed to play in a different theatre, were left homeless when it burned to the ground.

The Black Crook was playing at Biblo's Garden Theatre, and the manager decided to hire the 100 French dancers and incorporate them in the melodrama. At the same time, he hired their scenery and had a number of songs written.

The show was a riotous success overnight and ran for 474 performances in New York and for many years on tour!

THE MUSICAL was born.

Musical theatre had begun its long, and successful life. Constantly changing and recreating itself over time, musical theatre has historically incorporated styles of music that represent the current trend as well as pushing forward barriers and moving goal posts.

It is interesting to note that Sigmund Romberg, (see p.48) took the story of *The Black Crook* and used it as the inspiration for his 1954 Broadway show *The Girl In Pink Tights*.

Styles of musical

> operetta

> Princess Theatre musicals

> book musicals

> compilation musicals

> theme musicals

> music-hall

- ➤ vaudeville and burlesque

- ➤ variety

- ➤ extravaganza

- ➤ revue

Let us look at the different types of musical.

- ➤ **Operetta**

  - • small-scale opera on a light or humorous theme

Operetta is a form of musical theatre that tells a story. *The Merry Widow* by Franz Lehár (1905) is arguably the most famous operetta ever written and it is still popular today.

Many musical theatre performers find themselves in operetta companies – particularly on the continent now, where it is still a highly regarded recognised art form.

If you listen to some of the melodies in operetta works you will begin to recognise the musical form and style that is prevalent today in works by Lloyd-Webber or even Sondheim!

> **Princess Theatre Musicals**

- cohesive stories with songs fitting the characters and situations

It wasn't until a series of Broadway productions at the Princess Theater, the 'Princess Theatre Musicals' that the first attempts were made to offer modern, cohesive, funny, intimate stories – with songs that more or less fitted the characters and situations.

Many of these shows were written by a young composer, Jerome Kern, who later wrote *Showboat* (1927), which became one of the great landmarks in the history of the musical.

Showboat was influential because it led the way to the creation of a form of musical play that was distinct from fast moving, musical comedy on one hand and flamboyant operetta on the other. It was innovative because of its well-drawn characters, the strength of the story and the firmness with which the songs were wedded to the tale.

It wasn't until much later that another landmark

musical emerged and *Oklahoma!* was first produced at St James Theatre, New York on 31ˢᵗ March 1943. When Richard Rodgers and Oscar Hammerstein II wrote *Oklahoma!* the musical numbers were so closely interwoven with the text and plot that they advanced the story of the play.

It could be said that Rodgers and Hammerstein were leading the way for the 'through sung' musicals of today. Of course a through sung theatre piece is no stranger as it is seen and heard in a different form of theatre that we know as Opera!

If you are looking for unusual songs then explore the Princess Theatre Musicals such as *Very Good Eddie* (1915) and *Oh! Boy* (1917).

> **Book musicals**

- tell a story

This type of musical has been given the name because it tells a story like its forerunner operetta. Book musicals have a beginning, middle and an end.

The storyline can be:

- ➢ original

- ➢ inspired by the life of a person

- ➢ inspired by an idea

- ➢ inspired by a collection of poems

- ➢ based on a book

- ➢ based on a play that was based on a book

- ➢ based on a film

The book musical storyline can be original like *Rags* (Charles Strousse, 1987) or the musical can be based on a person like Eva Peron, for example (*Evita* by Andrew Lloyd Webber, 1978). The storyline can be based on a book like *Ragtime* (Ahrens & Flaherty, 1998) – an adaptation of E. L. Doctorow's American burlesque novel or based on a play that had been based on a book like *Cabaret* (Kander & Ebb, 1966) – the musical version of Christopher Isherwood's look at pre-war Berlin. The book musical can be based on a film *(The Full Monty* by McNally & Yazbek, 2000), inspired by an idea *(Follies* by Stephen Sondheim, 1971) or even inspired by a collection of poems! *Cats* (Andrew Lloyd Webber, 1981).

➤ Compilation musicals

- celebrate the work of a composer or lyricist

Compilation musicals celebrate the work of a composer or lyricist but don't tell a story. Examples include *Cowardy Custard* (1972) based on Noel Coward's music and lyrics and *Side By Side* (1976) based on the works of Sondheim – the foremost musical theatre composer of the last forty years. *Mama Mia!* (1999) is really a compilation musical, too, because it uses the music of Abba as the excuse for the show and only builds a very thin story around the music.

➤ Theme musicals

- have a theme instead of a storyline

Sometimes a composer might write a selection of songs and present them in a musical that doesn't have a storyline but has a theme running through it instead. Good examples of this type of musical are *Starting Here, Starting Now* by Maltby & Shire (1977) and *Songs For A New World* (1995) by Jason Robert Brown.

➤ Music-hall

- singers, comedians and speciality acts presided over by a chairman

Music-hall was a forerunner of the variety show. It started in inns and taverns in the 18th century and moved into theatres by the early 19th century. There were sometimes as many as 25 turns on the bill, ranging from speciality acts like acrobats and jugglers to comedians and singers, all presided over by a chairman. Famous music-hall entertainers include Florrie Forde: "I Do Like To Be Beside The Seaside" (written by the Edwardian composer John A. Glover-Kind) was one of her favourite songs. Vesta Victoria sang one of the most popular of all music-hall songs, "Waiting At The Church" (Fred Leigh and Henry Pether, 1906) and another top-of-the-bill music-hall artistes, Harry Champion, sang the 1911 showstopper "Any Old Iron" (music by Charles Collins and words by Fred Terry and A.E. Shepard). Charles Collins then combined with the lyricist Fred Leigh to write a favourite song of Marie Lloyd, "Don't Dilly Dally On The Way" in 1915.

Music-hall was extremely popular in its heyday, but it was killed off by the advent of the cinema, radio, and above all, television.

➢ Vaudeville and burlesque

- vaudeville: a collection of songs, sketches and speciality acts

- burlesque: a bawdy collection of songs, sketches and speciality acts including striptease

Of course, over the years many different sorts of 'musical theatre' have evolved around the world. In America there was vaudeville, a collection of songs, sketches and speciality acts. This was popular from about 1880 until the early 1930's and Al Jolson was one of the stars to emerge from it.

Burlesque was very similar but much more bawdy and sometimes included striptease artists as part of the entertainment. The Jule Styne musical *Gypsy* (lyrics by Stephen Sondheim) deals with the life story of one of the great striptease artists – Gypsy Rose Lee, and how she worked her way up from appearing in second-class burlesque shows to starring in the top extravaganzas and revues.

➢ Variety

- a mix of singers, dancers, comedians and speciality acts

Variety was a popular form of theatre entertainment for the first 70 years of the 20th century. A troupe of dancers and comedians padded out with speciality acts featured in the first half. Then, after the interval, it was time to see the 'top of the bill' with appearances by stars like Gracie Fields.

Gracie Fields had her London debut in 1915 and was firmly established by 1928. She first sang her theme tune "Sally" in 1931 and her sentimental songs and broad Lancashire humour won a unique place in the affections of British audiences.

At one time there were variety theatres all over the world but today, very few remain as working theatres. Sadly, most of them have been pulled down in the wake of the advent of television.

> **Extravaganza**

- A lavish spectacular production

An extravaganza represented the epitome of glamour with stunning costumes and scenery. The great producer Florenz Ziegfeld presented shows of this type in America from 1907–1931. These productions became known as *the Ziegfeld Follies.*

Ziegfeld himself has been the subject of many film and stage musicals and one or two stars of the *Ziegfeld Follies* have even had musicals written about their lives. *Funny Girl* (Jule Styne, 1966) is based on the Ziegfeld comedienne Fanny Brice and *The Will Rogers Follies* by Cy Coleman (1991) is based on the career of Will Rogers who was a great raconteur and performer of the time.

In America, Ziegfeld was the king of extravagant revue whereas England had the *Cochrane Revues* presented by the impresario Charles B. Cochrane. The chorus girls were known as Cochrane's Young Ladies; and many of the original chorus girls, such as Gertrude Lawrence, Anna Neagle and Jessie Matthews went on to become huge musical theatre stars in their own right.

➢ **Revue**

• short sketches, songs and dances

Another form of musical, which has now all but disappeared today, is revue, a light entertainment consisting of short sketches, songs and dances that has often focused on topical issues.

Revues were first seen in France in the 1820's and

the genre spread to Britain and America at the end of the 19th century. 20th century revues like *Blackbirds Of 1928* and *New Faces* introduced the world to a number of wonderful songs.

The Broadway revue *Blackbirds Of 1928* featured one of the greatest love songs ever written, "I Can't Give You Anything But Love (baby)" with words by one of the century's great lyricists, Dorothy Fields and music by Jimmy McHugh.

One if the most poignantly evocative songs about London, "A Nightingale Sang In Berkeley Square" (words by Eric Maschwitz and music by Manning Sherwing, 1940) was introduced by Judy Campbell in the wartime London musical revue, *New Faces*.

Revues were sometimes sophisticated in their content. For example, political revues or satirical revues focused on a specific subject like politics or took a satirical look at the life and times. One famous revue of this type was *Beyond The Fringe* written by and starring Peter Cook and Dudley Moore (1961).

Revues were not too far removed from the alternative television comedy shows we have today – although revues usually contained music, song and dance.

13   YOU HAVE ARRIVED AT DRAMA SCHOOL

So, you made it! Congratulations – you have arrived.

What now?

Remember, you might have been told by friends and family that you have a great talent and you might have got great reviews in your local paper for a performance at your local school or with an amateur dramatic company.

You might have been a big fish in a small pond.

Look around on day one of your training. There are probably other big fish – some who might have more talent than you and possibly some with less.

You now need to aspire to be the best in your peer group.

Investing in your course

You are about to start the most exciting and creative time of your life. You understand that the competition in the world of entertainment is great; and that in order to survive you have to gain the skills that are going to make you into a good performer.

DON'T waste your time at drama school.

- read plays and scripts

- see musicals, operas, plays and films

- practise and rehearse

You have got this far – DON'T lose your focus, passion and intent.

Get used to spending time outside your formal classes reading plays or scripts, seeing musicals, operas, plays and films, and constantly practise and rehearse what you are learning on a day-to-day basis.

Now the real hard work starts. If you thought that all the work you did in order to get your place was hard, then think again.

Remember, you are now at drama school – where you will probably have to unlearn some of the skills that you thought you were good at; and where you will be asked to lose 'baggage' that you have been carrying around (see Becoming a performer p.8).

Punctuality and discipline

One of the fundamental principles of being an actor is punctuality and personal discipline.

You will certainly need to present yourself at all your classes at drama school on time; and once you have entered the profession it is vital that you are dependable and punctual. If you are appearing in a stage musical, for example, you must be in the theatre by the 'half-hour' call at the latest.

The 'half-hour' call is made over the Tannoy to inform everyone that the curtain will go up in thirty-five minutes. When the 'quarter' (quarter-hour call) is announced it gives you twenty minutes before curtain up. The next call you hear will be the five – this means that you only have ten minutes. 'Overture and beginners' is the last call and it is at this point that you have to leave your dressing room and stand by for the start of the performance.

Discipline is vital – and your reputation will go before you.

It is never too soon to start thinking about your time management. Your days at drama school will be structured for you but your free time is something that you have to take responsibility for.

At the end of any day you might have to learn a sonnet, write an actors' journal, remember some dance moves, research a play, prepare a paper to discuss a playwright, be 'off the book' for a group singing class – ALL IN ONE EVENING!

Settle down; structure your evening of learning and save that social occasion for a later date! – when you know you can enjoy it without stress and tension.

DON'T burden yourself with unnecessary stress and tension because you haven't organised your life.

Noël Coward once asked a certain actress to be off the book for the following day's rehearsal. She thought she had learnt the lines but the next day it was obvious that she hadn't. The actress appealed to Coward saying, "I knew these lines backwards last night." to which he replied "yes, and that's exactly how you are saying them this morning"!

When you get your place at drama school don't throw it away!

Classes

You will attend all sorts of classes once you start

training and sometimes you will ask yourself what a particular class has to do with being an actor. This is usual! You will continually be asked to make connections between this class and that class and you might often find it difficult to comprehend why.

Most drama school students find this aspect irritating and difficult at first but as your training progresses it gets easier. Suddenly you will notice that a certain class can only happen once you've embraced another class that it draws upon.

You will be made aware of your spoken voice by the voice department – and the tutors might even ask you to find a different way of using this instrument that you have used in one way for the last eighteen years. There will be a reason for it and they will tell you why!

Your singing tutors might ask you to start singing in a totally different way from the one you have been used to – they will be exploring your potential and making the sound of your voice more acceptable and more pleasing and will probably work on your tone and pitch.

You will explore text and study playwrights like Chekhov and look at Stanislavsky's work in order to make you a better actor and give you a clearer picture of how to create, interpret and inhabit a character.

You will be taught group singing in order to be able to hold a harmony and you will probably be given the rudiments of notation to enable you to follow the music.

You will have classes in body conditioning, Alexander technique and commedia dell'arte. You might explore being an animal or playing trust games.

Stamina is a vital requisite of a good performer and dance classes will help you achieve this – you might even want to visit the local gym once or twice a week too, in order to build up your muscles.

In your first year there probably won't be an opportunity to do the one thing you came to drama school for . . . . . TO PERFORM. You will have to wait for that pleasure until you have got all your technical and physical training in order.

At drama school you will be expected to expose areas of your personal life, which at times might be difficult. Your tutors will be exploring and taking you to depths that you've probably never been in order to get deep down inside your emotions.

You will be asked to 'dig right down to the bottom of your soul' – and the importance of this is summed up perfectly in the song "Nothing" from *A Chorus Line* (Mavrin Hamlisch and Edward Kleban, 1975).

Make sure you dig – deep and hard!

If you have the talent, the stamina and perseverance and you've achieved success in all your disciplines while at drama school there is no reason why you shouldn't survive in the entertainment industry.

14   NOW YOU HAVE GRADUATED

You have been lucky enough to attend a drama school; and this should not only have allowed you to develop as a person but it should also have equipped you with the tools that you need to have a lasting career in the theatre industry.

Once you have graduated, that cosy little cushion that you've been sitting on for the last three years is suddenly pulled out from under you . . . . . and you find yourself on your own.

It is a frightening prospect – like the moment you pass your driving test and find yourself in the driving seat of a car with no one else there for the first time!

If you are lucky you might get a good agent when you graduate – but if you don't you will have to start marketing yourself.

It is possible that you will have to wait weeks or even months before you get your first audition. You must be prepared for this – DON'T loose heart.

NOTE: Show business is a serious business and managements will only invest in those actors who are going to give a return on the money invested.

Losing focus and determination

Here is a worst-case scenario that I've witnessed time and time again . . . . .

You graduate from drama school, with all your audition speeches and songs that you've worked so hard to put together, tucked neatly in a file; and you have spent time and money sending your photographs and c.v. to managements and casting directors.

However, when auditions aren't forthcoming you start to lose focus and determination – you even forget, or can't be bothered, to go through your audition pieces on a daily basis or continue your breathing and warm-up exercises.

Then, disaster . . . . . somehow or other, you mislay your file. Six months down the line the telephone rings and someone wants to audition you within a couple of hours.

You panic. Then, you eventually remember where your audition file is – but you can't remember your words. You have nothing clean and tidy to wear, you can't find your tap shoes and in all the panic of getting to the audition you find yourself running late.

You haven't even thought to ask who and what you

are auditioning for so you don't know which song or speech to deliver or the name of the person you will make contact with.

Eventually you arrive – probably late, looking nervous, appearing dishevelled and totally unprepared to audition!

Performers that get the jobs

Q   Who gets to work?

The performers who arrive on time, professionals who meet all the necessary requirements get to work.

Work goes to the talented performers with a professional attitude, and a confidence born of the ability to handle time management, together with the security of being thoroughly prepared.

These are the performers that get the jobs.

So remember, if you have something to sell, make sure that it comes in a package that people want to buy and that that package is available at all times!

You audition but don't get the job

Even if you are called for audition, you will not necessarily get the job.

When you have been called for audition but fail to land the job, you must learn to deal with your emotional response to the disappointment.

You probably won't get feedback on how well you did. You have no idea what the creative team thinks. They could all be saying, "That was a terrific audition. What a shame that person wasn't right for the part – but I'll certainly keep the person in mind next time I'm casting!"

Unfortunately, the feedback you are most likely to get is negative – when the telephone doesn't ring!

Musicals . . . . the world's most popular live entertainment.

Once you have opened the door to the world of musicals I can promise you a lifetime of exploration and research.

You will be introduced to brilliant composers and lyricists; you will be entranced by wonderful stories and, of course, you will hear some of the most breathtaking music that you will ever hear.

Hearing "You'll Never Walk Alone" (*Carousel*, Rodgers and Hammerstein, 1945) in a live theatre and not at a football match should inspire and challenge you to want to embrace the whole history of the musical.

You have chosen to play an active role in this world of musicals. As a performer it will be up to you to breathe new blood and life into the business we call show . . . . . .

. . . . . to play your own part in the continuing story of musicals and to celebrate **MUSICAL THEATRE**.

GOOD LUCK.

For details of Trinity College *London's* examinations in Musical Theatre contact:

> The Chief Examiner for Drama and Speech Subjects
> Trinity College *London*
> 89 Albert Embankment
> London
> SE1 7TP
>
> tel: +44 (0)20 7820 6100
> fax: +44 (0)20 7820 6161
> e-mail: info@trinitycollege.co.uk
> website: www.trinitycollege.co.uk

 Dramatic Lines publishers produce a wide range of material to help young performers and publish a number of Musical Theatre pieces suitable for Trinity College *London* group examinations.

> Dramatic Lines publishers
> PO Box 201
> Twickenham
> TW2 5RQ
>
> freephone orderline: 0800 5429570
> tel: +44 (0)20 8296 9502
> fax: +44 (0)20 8296 9503
> e-mail: mail@dramaticlinespublishers.co.uk
> website: www.dramaticlines.co.uk

Musicline Publications publish a wide range of musicals for schools, many with backing tracks.

Musicline Publications Ltd

5 Mill House

Tolsons Mill

Lichfield Street

Fazeley

Staffordshire

B78 3QD

tel: +44 (0)1827 707384

fax: +44 (0)1827 284214

e-mail: musicline@btopenworld.com

website: www.musicline-ltd.com

BIBLIOGRAPHY

Musicals
Michael Patrick Kennedy & John Muir
(Collins)

Musicals *(The complete illustrated story)*
Kurt Gänzl
(Carlton Books)

The Musical from Inside Out
Stephen Citron
(Hodder and Stoughton)

The Show Must Go On
Lin Marsh and Wendy Cook
(Faber Music)

The Guiness Who's Who of Stage Musicals
Colin Larkin (Ed)
(Guiness Publishing)

American Musical Theatre
Gerald Boardman
(Oxford University Press)

Opening Nights on Broadway
Steven Suskin
(Schirmer Books)

More Opening Nights On Broadway

Steven Suskin

(Schirmer Books)

Broadway Babies Say Goodnight *(Musicals then and now)*

Mark Steyn

(Faber and Faber)

Choreographing the Stage Musical

Margot Sutherland and Kenneth Pickering

(Garnet Miller)

Song By Song *(14 Great Lyric Writers)*

Caryl Brahms and Ned Sherrin

(Ross Anderson Publications)

DRAMATIC LINES HANDBOOKS in association with

Trinity, The International Examinations Board

MUSICAL THEATRE

ISBN 1 904557 12 0

Gerry Tebbutt

□

ACTING SHAKESPEARE FOR AUDITIONS AND EXAMINATIONS

ISBN 1 904557 10 4

Frank Barrie

□

SPEECH AND DRAMA

ISBN 1 904557 15 5

Ann Jones and Robert Cheeseman

□

THINKING ABOUT PLAYS

ISBN 1 904557 14 7

Ken Pickering and Giles Auckland-Lewis

□

PREPARING FOR YOUR DIPLOMA IN DRAMA AND SPEECH

ISBN 1 904557 11 2

Kirsty N Findlay and Ken Pickering

□

EFFECTIVE COMMUNICATION

ISBN 1 904557 13 9

John Caputo, Jo Palosaari and Ken Pickering

ADDITIONAL TITLES AVAILABLE

All books may be ordered direct from:

DRAMATIC LINES   PO BOX 201   TWICKENHAM   TW2 5RQ   ENGLAND

freefone: 0800 5429570
t: 020 8296 9503
f: 020 8296 9503
e: mail@dramaticlinespublishers.co.uk
www.dramaticlines.co.uk

MONOLOGUES

THE SIEVE
AND OTHER SCENES

Heather Stephens
ISBN 0 9522224 0 X

The Sieve contains unusual short original monologues valid for junior acting examinations. The material in The Sieve has proved popular with winning entries worldwide in drama festival competitions. Although these monologues were originally written for the 8-14 year age range they have been used by adult actors for audition and performance pieces. Each monologue is seen through the eyes of a young person with varied subject matter including tough social issues such as fear, 'Television Spinechiller', senile dementia , 'Seen Through a Glass Darkly' and withdrawal from the world in 'The Sieve'. Other pieces include: 'A Game of Chicken', 'The Present', 'Balloon Race' and a widely used new adaptation of Hans Christian Andersen's 'The Little Match Girl' in monologue form.

CABBAGE
AND OTHER SCENES

Heather Stephens
ISBN 0 9522224 5 0

Following the success of The Sieve, Heather Stephens has written an additional book of monologues with thought provoking and layered subject matter valid for junior acting examinations. The Cabbage monologues were originally written for the 8-14 year age range but have been used by adult actors for audition and performance pieces. The Aberfan slag heap disaster issues are graphically confronted in 'Aberfan Prophecy' and 'The Surviving Twin' whilst humorous perceptions of life are observed by young people in 'The Tap Dancer' and 'Cabbage'. Other pieces include: 'The Dinner Party Guest', 'Nine Lives' and a new adaptation of Robert Browning's 'The Pied Piper' seen through the eyes of the crippled child.

ALONE IN MY ROOM
ORIGINAL MONOLOGUES

Ken Pickering
ISBN 0 9537770 0 6

This collection of short original monologues includes extracts from the author's longer works in addition to the classics. Provocative issues such as poverty and land abuse are explored in 'One Child at a Time', 'The Young Person Talks' and 'Turtle Island' with adaptations from 'Jane Eyre', Gulliver's Travels' and 'Oliver Twist' and well loved authors include Dostoyevsky. These monologues have a wide variety of applications including syllabus recommendation for various acting examinations. Each monologue has a brief background description and acting notes.

DUOLOGUES

PEARS

Heather Stephens
ISBN 0 9522224 6 9

These thought provoking and unusual short original duologues provide new material for speech and drama festival candidates in the 8-14 year age range. The scenes have also been widely used for junior acting examinations and in a variety of school situations and theatrical applications. Challenging topics in Pears include the emotive issues of child migration, 'Blondie', 'The Outback Institution' and bullying 'Bullies', other scenes examine friendship, 'The Best of Friends', 'The Row' and envy, 'Never the Bridesmaid'. New adaptations of part scenes from 'Peace' by Aristophanes and 'Oliver Twist' by Charles Dickens are also included.

TOGETHER NOW
ORIGINAL DUOLOGUES

Ken Pickering
ISBN 0 9537770 1 4

This collection of short duologues includes extracts from Ken Pickering's longer works together with new original pieces. The variety of experiences explored in the scenes can all be easily identified with, such as an awkward situation, 'You Tell Her', and the journey of self knowledge in 'Gilgamesh', whilst 'Mobile phones', 'Sales' and 'Food' observe realistic situations in an interesting and perceptive way. Other duologues based on well known stories include 'Snow White' and 'The Pilgrim's Progress'. Each piece has a brief background description and acting notes. The scenes have syllabus recommendation for a number of examination boards and wide variety of theatrical and school applications.

SHAKESPEARE THE REWRITES
Claire Jones
ISBN 0 9522224 8 5

A collection of short monologues and duologues for female players. The scenes are from rewrites of Shakespeare plays from 1670 to the present day written by authors seeking to embellish original texts for performances, to add prequels or sequels or satisfy their own very personal ideas about production. This material is fresh and unusual and will provide exciting new audition and examination material. Comparisons with the original Shakespeare text are fascinating and this book will provide a useful contribution to Theatre Study work from GCSE to beyond 'A' level. Contributors include James Thurber (Macbeth) Arnold Wesker (Merchant of Venice) and Peter Ustinov (Romanoff and Juliet). The collection also includes a most unusual Japanese version of Hamlet.

RESOURCES

DRAMA LESSONS IN ACTION
Antoinette Line
ISBN 0 9522224 2 6

Resource material suitable for classroom and assembly use for teachers of junior and secondary age pupils. Lessons are taught through improvisation, these are not presented as 'model lessons' but provide ideas for adaptation and further development. Lessons include warm-up and speech exercises and many themes are developed through feelings such as timidity, resentfulness, sensitivity and suspicion. Material can be used by groups of varying sizes and pupils are asked to respond to texts from a diverse selection of well known authors including: Roald Dahl, Ogden Nash, John Betjeman, Ted Hughes, Michael Rosen, and Oscar Wilde.

AAARGH TO ZIZZ
Graeme Talboys
135 DRAMA GAMES
ISBN 0 9537770 5 7

This valuable resource material has been created by a drama teacher and used mostly in formal drama lessons but also in informal situations such as clubs and parties. The games are extremely flexible, from warm up to cool down, inspiration to conclusion and from deadly serious to purest fun and the wide variety ranges from laughing and rhythm activities to building a sentence and word association. Many games could be used as part of a PSHE programme together with activities connected with 'fair play'. The games are easily adapted and each has notes on setting up details of straightforward resources needed. All this material has been used with a wide range of young people in the 10 - 18 year age range.

DRAMA•DANCE•SINGING
TEACHER RESOURCE BOOK

edited by John Nicholas
ISBN 0 9537770 2 2

This collection of drama, dance and singing lesson activities has been drawn from a bank of ideas used by the Stagecoach Theatre Arts Schools teachers. Clearly presented lessons include speech and drama exercises, games and improvisations often developed as a response to emotions. Dance activities include warm-ups, basic dance positions, improvisations, versatile dance exercises and routines while singing activities help to develop rhythm and notation as well as providing enjoyable games to develop the voice. Activities can be easily adapted for large or small group use and are suitable for 6 - 16 year olds in a fun yet challenging way.

MUSICAL PLAYS

THREE CHEERS FOR MRS BUTLER   adapted by Vicky Ireland
ISBN 0 9537770 4 9

This versatile musical play about everyday school life is for anyone who has ever been to school. It features the poems and characters created by Allan Ahlberg with a foreword by Michael Rosen, songs by Colin Matthews and Steven Markwick and was first performed at the Polka Theatre for Children, London. The two acts of 40 minutes each can be performed by children, adults or a mixture of both and the play can be produced with a minimum cast of 7 or a large cast of any size, with or without music and songs, as well as having a wide variety of other musical and dramatic applications.

INTRODUCING OSCAR
The Selfish Giant & The Happy Prince

Veronica Bennetts
ISBN 0 9537770 3 0

Oscar Wilde's timeless stories for children have been chosen for adaptation because of the rich opportunities offered for imaginative exploration and the capacity to vividly illuminate many aspects of the human condition. The original dialogue, lyrics and music by Veronica Bennetts can be adapted and modified according to the needs of the pupils and individual schools or drama groups. The Selfish Giant runs for 25 minutes and The Happy Prince for 1 hour 15 minutes. Both musical can be used for Trinity College, *London*. examinations and are ideal for end of term productions, for drama groups and primary and secondary schools.

WHAT IS THE MATTER WITH MARY JANE?   Wendy Harmer
ISBN 0 9522224 4 2

This monodrama about a recovering anorexic and bulimic takes the audience into the painful reality of a young woman afflicted by eating disorders. The play is based on the personal experience of actress Sancia Robinson and has proved hugely popular in Australia. It is written with warmth and extraordinary honesty and the language, humour and style appeal to current youth culture. A study guide for teachers and students is included in this English edition ensuring that the material is ideal for use in the secondary school classroom and for PSHE studies, drama departments in schools and colleges in addition to amateur and professional performance.

X-STACY
Margery Forde
ISBN 0 9522224 9 3

Margery Forde's powerful play centres on the rave culture and illicit teenage drug use and asks tough questions about family, friends and mutual responsibilities. The play has proved hugely successful in Australia and this English edition is published with extensive teachers' notes by Helen Radian, Lecturer of Drama at Queensland University of Technology, to enrich its value for the secondary school classroom, PSHE studies, English and drama departments.

ASSEMBLIES! ASSEMBLIES! ASSEMBLIES!   Kryssy Hurley
ISBN 0 9537770 6 5

These teacher-led assemblies require minimum preparation and have been written by a practising teacher to involve small or large groups. Each assembly lasts 15-20 minutes and is suitable for Key Stages 2 and 3. There are 12 for each term and these explore many PSHE and Citizenship issues including bullying, racism, friendship, co-operation, feeling positive, making responsible choices and decisions, school rules and laws outside school. All have the following sections: *Resource and Organisation, What To Do, Reflection Time and Additional Resources and Activities.*

JELLY BEANS Joseph McNair Stover
ISBN 0 9522224 7 7

The distinctive style and deceptively simple logic of American writer Joseph McNair Stover has universal appeal with scenes that vary in tone from whimsical to serious and focus on young peoples relationships in the contemporary world. The 10 to 15 minute original scenes for 2, 3, and 4 players are suitable for 11 year old students through to adult. Minimal use of sets and props makes Jelly Beans ideal for group acting examinations, classroom drama, assemblies, and a wide variety of additional theatrical applications.

SCENES 4 3 2 10 PLAYERS Sandy Hill
ISBN 0 9537770 8 1

There are 10 original scenes in the book written for 3 to 10 players with opportunities for doubling-up of characters and introduction of optional additional players. The versatile scenes are of varying playing times and are suitable for performers from as young as 7 through to adult. The flexible use of sets and props have made these pieces particularly useful for group acting examinations and have proved to be immediately popular and successful for candidates as well as winning entries at drama festivals, they can also be used effectively for classroom drama and school assemblies. The scenes are often quirky and vary in tone with unusual endings. They will be enjoyed by performers and audiences alike.

WILL SHAKESPEARE SAVE US! Paul Nimmo
WILL SHAKESPEARE SAVE THE KING! ISBN 0 9522224 1 8

Two versatile plays in which famous speeches and scenes from Shakespeare are acted out as part of a comic story about a bored king and his troupe of players. These plays are suitable for the 11-18 year age range and have been produced with varying ages within the same cast and also performed by adults to a young audience. The plays can be produced as a double bill, alternatively each will stand on its own, performed by a minimum cast of 10 without a set, few props and modern dress or large cast, traditional set and costumes. The scripts are ideal for reading aloud by classes or groups and provide an excellent introduction to the works of Shakespeare. Both plays have been successfully performed on tour and at the Shakespeare's Globe in London.

SUGAR ON SUNDAYS
AND OTHER PLAYS

Andrew Gordon
ISBN 0 9522224 3 4

A collection of six one act plays bringing history alive through drama. History is viewed through the eyes of ordinary people and each play is packed with details about everyday life, important events and developments of the period. The plays can be used as classroom drama, for school performances and group acting examinations and also as shared texts for the literacy hour. The plays are suitable for children from Key Stage 2 upwards and are 40-50 minutes in length and explore Ancient Egypt, Ancient Greece, Anglo-Saxon and Viking Times, Victorian Britain and the Second World War. A glossary of key words helps to develop children's historical understanding of National Curriculum History Topics and the plays provide opportunities for children to enjoy role play and performance.